SELF CONFIDENCE AND SELF-ESTEEM

Boost your mental toughness, social skills and obtain the life you dream of

EXTENDED VERSION

EMMA CAMPBELL

TABLE OF CONTENTS

INTRODUCTION

Lack of self-confidence and self-esteem—though may differ in meaning—the duo have come to become a major force to be reckoned with in the lives of millions of people around the world with their innate abilities to hinder basic day to day living, causing many to fall into vicious cycles of depression, anxiety, stress, self-consciousness, and genuine unfulfillment. This leaves many of its victims not to lead their "best life" as it were. They barely struggle to get by each day; without having to stand up to anyone (most likely a bully), without having any reason to accept a compliment because they believe they don't deserve it, or even just having to go through the thought of whether they're "good enough" because, in their thoughts, they simply aren't.

So, this book is aimed at understanding the concepts of self-confidence, self-esteem, and its intricacies. We'll also look at how to acquire these extraordinary skills and apply them in our daily life so we can boost our mental toughness, social skills, and acquire the life we've always dreamed of.

It's the writer's desire that, by the end of this book, you have gone from being a victim to acquiring the knowledge and skills you need to become the best version of yourself; the one you were always meant to be.

SECTION 1- ROAD TO SELF-CONFIDENCE

CHAPTER 1
BUILDING CONFIDENCE

Confidence isn't something that can be similar to a lot of rules; confidence is a perspective. Constructive reasoning, being prepared, acquiring information, and conversing with others are valuable approaches to help improve or support your confidence levels.

Confidence originates from sentiments of prosperity, acknowledgment of your body and psyche (your confidence), and faith in your capacity, aptitudes, and experience. Confidence is a quality that many people might want to have.

What is Self-Confidence?

Though self-confidence can mean various things to various individuals, in actuality, it essentially implies having confidence in yourself.

Confidence is, to a limited extent, an aftereffect of how we have been raised and how we've been instructed. We gain from others how to consider ourselves and how to carry on. These exercises influence what we accept about ourselves and others. Confidence is also an aftereffect of our encounters and how we've figured out how to respond to various circumstances.

Self-confidence is certifiably not a static measure. Our confidence to perform jobs and assignments and manage circumstances can increment and decline, and a few days we may feel surer than others.

Low-confidence can be an aftereffect of numerous components including fear of the obscure, analysis, being discontent with individual appearance, feeling ill-equipped, poor time, absence of information, and past disappointments. When we regularly need trust in ourselves, it is a result of what we accept others will consider us. Maybe others will snicker, grumble, or commit fun about us on the off chance that we make an error. Thinking like this can keep us from doing things we need or want to do simply because we accept that the results are excessively difficult or humiliating.

Carelessness can be an issue because it causes you to accept that you can do anything regardless of whether you don't have the vital aptitudes, capacities, and information to do it well. In such circumstances, carelessness can prompt disappointment. Being excessively sure implies you are bound to run over to others as presumptuous or self-absorbed. Individuals are significantly more prone to enjoy your disappointment if you are seen in this light.

Confidence and self-esteem are not similar, even though they are frequently connected. Confidence is a certain region.

Playing out a job or finishing an errand isn't about not committing errors. Slip-ups are unavoidable, particularly while exploring new territory. Confidence incorporates comprehending what to do when errors become known and is also about critical thinking and dynamics.

Self-Confidence Vs. Self-Esteem
The term esteem is coined from the word estimate, which means to grade yourself on a standard. Self-esteem means to evaluate your value and impact in your professional and personal life. If you consider yourself important to the people around you, are contributing

to the development of your surroundings, and are an indispensable asset in other people's lives, then you could say that you have high self-esteem.

In other words, someone with high self-esteem thinks he is worthy of the world he is in and understands his significance. While self-esteem is dependent on the perception of self, self-confidence is entirely different.

Self-confidence, on the other hand, is affiliated to action and is more domain-specific. It is not an absolute observation as self-esteem, just the way self-esteem is thinking of your worth in relation to the world. On the contrary, self-confidence is your positive self-assessment in carrying out a task.

Someone who is confident of his abilities in one task, might not be certain when given another. Hence, self-confidence depends on the task given to perform and on your own ability to do so.

Dynamics of Self-Confidence
Now that we have gotten a grasp on how self-confidence depends on your perceived ability to manage an action, let's talk about the actions that help cultivate a sense of self-confidence. Self-confidence thrives in an atmosphere where the person is provided constructive feedback and the attention is always on the positive.

In such a working environment, a confident individual will be able to express his skills and talents beyond expectation, as he will get an opportunity to set goals, forget his past mistakes, and learn new things.

However, a self-confidence person can be seriously hindered in an environment where there is consistent comparison with others and where expectations are unrealistic. People are pitted against one another per their performance in the numbers game.

In these conditions, an individual will be forced to nurture an unhealthy competitive mentality by resorting to under-handed means for success, listening to unworthy role models, being too stern in judging his performances, and underestimating his capabilities.

Such an environment breeds an unhealthy workplace where the stress is more on over-shadowing one anothers performance, as opposed to coming together as a team to assist one another. Such companies might rise for a while, but they ultimately crash.

Traits of Self-Confident People
Individuals with high self-confidence approach their issues differently when compared to others. They know the significance of building relationships and they cherish meeting new people to get and share new ideas. This quality of theirs is what makes them likable, as they are always willing to be in a conversation that gives equal importance and respect to all participants. Confident people enjoy expressing their ideas in front of others since they are emotionally capable to take constructive criticisms and reject emotional ones. That doesn't make them arrogant; on the contrary, they give everyone the chance to put their points forth. However, they have the courage to stick to their decision regardless of a lot of opposition to their ideas, if they are convinced they are doing the right thing.

There are two possible outcomes to any decision taken: either it turns out to be the right one, or you fail. However, what sets apart a confident person is that he doesn't boss around on detractors when he succeeds.

Also, a self-confident person is not too proud to acknowledge his mistakes and learn from them when he is wrong. This objective approach towards both success and failure is what makes a confident individual a lovable and respectable personality.

Traits of Under-Confident People
When compared with people of high self-confidence, people with low self-confidence have a very harsh and critical view of themselves. They are more likely to make emotional decisions as opposed to thinking rationally. They tend to be in their 'caves' instead of interacting with new people. They attempt to shun new company and avoid meeting new people.

An under-confident person tends to feel that he has nothing important or constructive to add to any process. This feeling of low self-worth, combined with an utter denial towards any change, makes an under-confident person extremely susceptible to mistreatment and undervaluation.

People with low confidence hesitate in expressing their thoughts and opinions since they think their views will be made fun of in public. In addition to this, their past experiences and interactions with people have not done anything to improve their self-worth and change their views about their productivity and importance.

It's at this point that a productive atmosphere comes into play. Everyone learns from his surroundings and your self-confidence depends directly on the type of people you meet and the type of interactions you have with them. While self-confident people interact with people who have something to learn or gain from, under-confident people are convinced that they can't change and are going to be undervalued in spite of what they do.

Approaches to Improve Confidence

There are different sides to improving confidence. Even though a definitive point is to feel progressively positive about yourself and your capacities, it is worth thinking about how you appear to others. The accompanying rundown has thoughts about the most proficient method to accomplish this.

Arranging and Preparation
Individuals frequently feel less certain about new or conceivably troublesome circumstances. Maybe the most significant factor in creating confidence is arranging and getting ready for the obscure. If you are going after another position, it would be a smart thought to prepare for the meeting. Plan what you would need to state and think about a portion of the inquiries that might be posed. Practice your answers with companions or associates and listen to their criticism.

There are numerous different instances of making arrangements for a meeting. Maybe you should visit the beautician before you go? How are you going to go to the meeting and to what extent will the excursion take? What would be advisable for you to wear? Assume responsibility for obscure circumstances as well as to be expected, separate errands into smaller sub-assignments, and plan the greatest number possible.

In certain circumstances, it might also be important to have alternate courses of action. Reinforce your plans if your arrangement falls flat.

For instance, if you intended to venture out to your meeting via car that very morning and the car wouldn't start, how would you get there? Having the option to respond with tranquility to the startling predicament is an indication of confidence.

Learning, Knowledge, and Training
Learning and research can assist us with feeling certain about our capacity to deal with circumstances, jobs, and assignments.

Recognizing what's in store and how and why things are done will add to your mindfulness and as a rule, it will cause you to feel organized and sure of yourself.

Be that as it may, learning and picking up information can cause us to feel less sure about our capacities to perform jobs and undertakings. When this happens, we have to consolidate our insight with experience. By accomplishing something, we have taken in a great deal about how we put the hypothesis to practice, which creates confidence and adds to our learning and understanding.

First-time guardians may feel anxious and not exactly certain about having an infant. They will probably purchase books or visit sites that can offer counsel and dissipate a portion of secrets. They are also liable to talk with different guardians to pick up information.

In the work environment, preparing might be given to staff to show them how to oversee or function with new frameworks and strategies. During a time of hierarchical change, this is especially significant since the same number of individuals will normally oppose changes. If those who are influenced by the progressions are given sufficient data and preparation, at that point such protections can, and for the most part, be limited as the staff feels arranged and subsequently certain with the new framework.

Positive Ideas Can be an Amazing Method For Improving Confidence
If you accept you can accomplish something, you are probably going to make a solid effort to ensure you do assume, in any case, that you don't accept how you can achieve an errand. In doing so, you are bound to move toward it pitifully and be bound to fall flat. The stunt is persuading yourself that you can accomplish something with the correct assistance, backing, readiness, and information.

Positive thinking is the confidence that prompts accomplishment. There is no hope without expectation and confidence.

There is a great deal of data about positive reasoning both on the web and in print. The fundamental principles of positive believing are to feature your qualities, victories, and gain from your shortcomings and errors. This is simpler than it sounds, and we regularly mention about things that we are not content with. We make them into greater issues than what they should be. These negative considerations can be harmful to confidence and your capacity to accomplish objectives.

Attempt to Recondition the Manner with Which You Consider Your Life
Know your qualities and shortcomings. Compose a rundown of things that you accept and things that you know you need improvement in. Talk about your rundown with loved ones as they will have the option to add to the rundown. Celebrate and build up your qualities and discover approaches to improve or deal with your shortcomings.

We always commit errors. Try not to think about your mix-ups as negatives, yet rather as learning openings.

Acknowledge praises and praise yourself. When you get a commendation from another person, say thanks to them and request more subtleties; what precisely did they like? Perceive your accomplishments and praise them by remunerating yourself and informing your loved ones about them.

Use analysis as a learning experience. Everyone sees the world in their way, from their point of view, and what works for one individual may not work for another. An analysis is only the assessment of another person. Be assertive while getting analysis, don't answer in a guarded way or let analysis bring you down with your confidence. Tune in to the analysis and ensure that you comprehend what is being said so you can utilize analysis as an approach to learn and improve.

Attempt to remain commonly bright and have an uplifting point of view. Offer others praises and salute them on their triumphs.

Converse with Others and Follow Their Lead
Get yourself a good confidence example.

In a perfect world, this will be somebody that you see routinely, a work associate, a relative, or a companion; someone with a great deal of self-assurance who you'd prefer to reflect. Watch them and notice how they carry on when they are being certain. How would they move, how would they talk, what do they say and when? How would they act when confronted with an issue or mix-up? How would they communicate with others and how would others respond to them?

Converse with them to get familiar with how they think and what is most important to them. By addressing and being around individuals who are confident it will, for the most part, help you to feel sure about yourself. Gain from other people who are fruitful in satisfying the errands and objectives that you wish to accomplish. Let their confidence rub off on you.

As you become convinced at that point offer assistance and exhortation, become a good example for someone less sure.

Confidence is contagious. So is the absence of it.

Experience
As we effectively complete undertakings and objectives, our confidence that we can finish the equivalent and comparative assignments increases.

A straightforward case of this is driving a vehicle. Many people who have been driving for quite a while do so consequently. They don't need to consider which hawk to push or how to deal with an intersection in the street, they get it done. This differentiates a student driver who will likely feel anxious and need to think hard. The student needs experience and trust in their capacity to drive, which they need to build up over time.

Picking up an understanding and venturing out, in any case, will be extremely troublesome. The idea of beginning something new is more regrettable than really doing it. This is the place planning, learning, and thinking that can help.

Separate jobs and errands into little feasible objectives make every single one of your objectives fit the SMART measures. That is to make objectives Specific, Measurable, Attainable, Realistic and Timed.

Whatever you do, expect to become as great as could reasonably be expected. The better you are at accomplishing something, the surer you will become.

Be Assertive
Being assertive means defending what you have faith in and adhering to your standards.

Being assertive also implies that you can adjust your perspective if you trust it as a proper activity, not because you are feeling the squeeze from another person.

Assertiveness, confidence, and esteem are firmly connected. Individuals normally become assertive as they build up their confidence.

Resist The Urge to Panic
There is a relationship between confidence and tranquility. If you feel sure about an assignment, at that point, you will probably feel confident about doing it. At the point when you feel less certain, you are bound to be pushed or apprehensive.

To abstain from freezing when you're feeling pressured, a rule will cause you to feel progressively sure.

To do this, it is valuable to figure out how to unwind. Learn any unwinding methods that work for you and how you can utilize it in case you're feeling focused. This might be as straightforward as taking some conscious exhales and inhales.

Maintain A Strategic Distance From Arrogance
Egotism is averse to relational connections.

As your confidence develops and you become effective, abstain from feeling or acting better than others. Keep in mind; no one is great and there is more that you can learn. Praise your qualities and triumphs, and perceive your shortcomings and disappointments. Give others kudos for their work. Use praises and acclaim earnestly. Be affable and courteous, show enthusiasm for what others are doing, pose inquiries, and get included.

Admit to your slip-ups and be set up to snicker at yourself!

Building Up Your Self-Confidence Skills
Confidence can reduce after some time if you don't rehearse your abilities or if you hit setbacks. As you become more assertive you should keep on rehearsing your aptitudes to help keep you up and help your confidence further. Focus on your confidence and step out of your customary range of familiarity and do things that cause you to feel a level of anxiety or trepidation.

Potential confidence targets may include:

- Start an undertaking or venture that you've been procrastinating for quite a while. Regularly we put off beginning significant assignments since they appear to be overpowering, troublesome, or too hard to finish. Causing a beginning on such an undertaking to help with confidence will make you more assertive to finish it.

- Submit a question in a café if there is an issue with your request. If you wouldn't grumble about an issue, at that point doing so is a decent method to improve your confidence and self-esteem aptitudes.

- Stand up and pose an inquiry at an open gathering or in a gathering. By doing this you are making yourself the focal point of consideration for a couple of moments.

- Volunteer to give an introduction or deliver a discourse. For some, individuals addressing a gathering of people is an especially startling possibility. The most ideal approach is to beat this dread and increase confidence with experience.

- Acquaint yourself with another person. This could be someplace where individuals share something for all intents and purposes, like at a gathering or a meeting, making it conceivably simpler to have a discussion. Or, on the other hand, you could converse with a total outsider in a lift.

- Wear something that will draw consideration, for example, a conspicuous bit of clothing. Individual appearance is a significant factor in confidence and individuals with lower confidence will make an effort not to be taken note of. Say something and captivate everyone!

- Join a gathering or class in your local proximity. You will profit from multiple points of view by meeting new people and learn new things while improving your confidence.

- Take a new excursion in an open vehicle. Venturing out to another spot and utilizing a new course with different people will cause the vast majority to feel marginally awkward.

What is your opinion about every one of the thoughts on the rundown above? Maybe some gave you minor sentiments of butterflies while others filled you with fear. Even though the rundown utilizes regular instances of confidence-boosting undertakings, none might directly affect you. Think about some confidence choices that focus on what is for you. Start with simpler ones, then develop yourself.

CHAPTER 2

POSITIVE SELF IMAGE

We are assaulted each day with images of flawlessness: immaculate lives, impeccable bodies, immaculate youngsters, all held up for investigation by utilizing web-based life.

These images are difficult to satisfy, so maybe it is no big surprise that foundations caution that psychological well-being issues are rising, particularly among youngsters.

It is, nonetheless, conceivable to find a way to secure yourself against the surge of flawlessness.

One important weapon to create is a positive self-image, an acknowledgment of your body. The two are great and awful focuses but encourages you to get certain and okay with yourself.

What Is Self-Image?

Self-image is how you truly see yourself, both when you consider yourself, and when you look in a mirror.

Self-image is influenced by how you feel about your body, including tallness, weight, and shape. Your convictions about your appearance, which may incorporate perspectives about the 'right' appearance; and how your physical body feels to you as you move.

Self-image is also influenced by generalizations and convictions, including those of the individuals around you just as your own.

Having a positive self-image doesn't imply that you ponder how your body is great.

With all things considered, no one is great, not in any case.

Rather, positive self-image implies tolerating your body for what it is, commending your regular shape and size, and how your body performs.

Individuals with a positive self-image comprehend how their appearance has nothing to do with capacity or character. They are sure and right about themselves and don't sit around idly stressing over their body.

Building Up A Positive Body Image
Building up a positive self-image, or helping another person to do as such, requires three key abilities or qualities:

1. Great Self-Esteem

Self-image is firmly connected to self-esteem, which is how you feel about your capacities, and can be the best idea of your 'inward voice'.

Those with low self-esteem may also have a negative image of their bodies since they have a low assessment of themselves and their capacities. Both are also connected to self-confidence.

Improving your self-esteem requires developing your perspective on yourself. It implies assuming responsibility for your inward exchange and guaranteeing that it turns out to be positive. Rather than concentrating on what may turn out badly, it is critical to concentrate on what is now acceptable.

2. A Positive Demeanor

The subsequent component—a positive mentality—is firmly connected to self-esteem.

Positive reasoning is the possibility that you can transform yourself by speculation more positively. If this sounds somewhat fleecy and non-logical, consider the placebo impact, a notable case of the intensity of positive reasoning.

The Placebo Effect
The placebo impact is a wonderly observation in clinical preliminaries and in different trials of new medications. Clinical preliminaries include three gatherings of patients: one given the new medication, a second given something that appears as though it is the new medication, however, has no impact (a placebo), and the third given no new medication by any stretch of the imagination.

Specialists regularly notice that the patients offered the non-successful medication show hints of progress. This has been archived again and again. There is no clinical explanation behind this improvement. (the medication that they are being given can't cause these impacts since it contains no dynamic fixings.) The main end is that these patients improve because they accept they are being given something that will improve them.

This is the placebo effect and it shows the intensity of the brain.

Three reasonable approaches to assist you with avoiding creating negative perspectives on your body, and help you to think more positively are:

1. Attempt to Maintain A Strategic Distance from Hairsplitting

No one is great, and attempting to be impeccable in any circle is just going to prompt issues in the long haul. Sufficient is adequate.

2. Try Not to Make Examinations

It is anything but difficult to fall into the snare of contrasting your life or your body with others, and imagining that yours is substandard in one way or another. Internet-based life makes this particularly likely because of the vast majority of people who are introducing curated images of their lives, intended to look superior to the truth. Stay away from correlations, and attempt to just commend on others' triumphs just like your own.

3. Maintain A Strategic Distance From The Compulsion to Scrutinize or Pass Judgment

It is in every case simple to scrutinize. Sadly, being profoundly basic is somewhat of a propensity, and once you begin to utilize this methodology with others, it will bounce back on you. A feeling of equity is acceptable, yet you also need to give everybody, including yourself, a break every now and again. Not racing to judge is going to make you kinder and more pleasant to be near.

4. Emotional Mindfulness and Self-Control is called Emotional Dependability

At last, to deal with your perspectives about your body, you should know and be in charge of your emotions.

There will be times when you see or hear things that will disturb you, and influence your perspective on your body. On these occasions, you should have the option to comprehend what you are feeling, and why, to assist you with overseeing and beat those sentiments, while maintaining a strategic distance from them from influencing your self-image consistently.

A Few Exercises to Help Grow Better A Self-Image

- If you are attempting to build up a positive image of your body, you may discover a portion of these exercises help.

- Make a rundown of the considerable number of things that your body encourages you to do, from the basics like breathing through to doing activities and getting you to the places you need to go, or to see the individuals you love. Help yourself to remember all the things that you were unable to manage without your body, and commend it for what it accomplishes for you.

- Make a rundown of ten things that you truly like about yourself (not identified with your appearance), and advise yourself that your appearance doesn't influence what your identity is.

- Surround yourself with positive individuals—individuals who like themselves, and who help you to do the same. If you invest your energy with individuals who are continually bringing themselves and you down, at that point, you will begin to feel that it is valid. Positive reasoning is all about getting, yet so is a negative mentality.

- Wear garments that you like and cause you to feel certain. Confidence radiates through by the way you stand and move and is gigantically alluring.

- Care for yourself. Give yourself a treat by heading off to some-place pleasant, or investing energy to accomplish something you love. Make sure to esteem yourself and commend your-self.

The Reality

A poor or negative self-image can be the beginning stage for genuine dysfunctional behaviors, including dietary problems like anorexia, just as nervousness and gloom. Building and keeping up a positive self-image along these lines is significant.

Figuring out how to acknowledge yourself and your body—or even just to offer yourself a reprieve once in a while—is one of the most significant individual aptitudes for the brain.

CHAPTER 3

ASSERTIVENESS

Assertiveness is a skill normally alluded to in social and relational skill training.

Being assertive means having the option to support your own or other's privileges quietly and positively without being either aggressive or latently tolerated as 'incorrect'.

Assertive people can express what is on their mind without upsetting others, or turning out to be vexed themselves.

Even though everybody demonstrates passive and aggressive manners every now and again, such methods for reacting regularly result from an absence of confidence and are, in this manner, improper methods for cooperating with others.

This page analyzes the rights and duties of conduct and expects to show how assertiveness can profit you.

What Is Assertiveness?

The Concise Oxford Dictionary characterizes assertiveness as:

'Direct, positive, emphasis on the acknowledgment of one's privileges'

At the end of the day, assertiveness implies supporting your privileges, communicating musings, emotions, and convictions in immediate, legitimate, and suitable ways.

It is critical to note that by being assertive we ought to consistently regard the musings, sentiments, and convictions of others.

The individuals who carry on assertiveness consistently regard the considerations, sentiments, and convictions of others just as their own.

Assertiveness concerns having the option to communicate sentiments, wishes, needs, and wants properly, and it is a significant individual and relational expertise. In the entirety of your connections with others, regardless of whether at home or work, with businesses, clients or partners, assertiveness can assist you with expressing yourself in an unmistakable, open and sensible way, without sabotaging your own or others privileges.

Assertiveness empowers people to act in their eventual benefits, to go to bat for themselves without undue nervousness, to communicate fair emotions serenely, and to communicate individual rights without preventing the rights from claiming others.

Assertive, Passive, and Aggressive
Assertiveness is regularly observed as the parity point among detached and aggressive conduct, however, it's most likely simpler to think about the three as purposes of a triangle.

Being Assertive
Being confident includes thinking about your own and other's privileges, wishes, needs, and wants.

Assertiveness implies urging others to be transparent about their perspectives, wishes, and sentiments, with the goal that the two gatherings act properly.

Assertive conduct incorporates:

- Being open in communicating wishes, contemplations, and emotions while urging others to do the same.

- Tuning in to the perspectives of others and reacting fittingly, regardless of whether in concurrence with those perspectives or not.

- Tolerating duties and having the option to delegate to other people.

- Routinely communicate valuation for others for what they have done or are doing.

- Having the option to confess to mistakes and apologize.

- Keeping up poise.

- Carrying on as an equivalent to other people.

A few people may battle to carry on assertively for various reasons and find that they act either aggressively or inactively.

Being Passive
Reacting in an uninvolved or non-assertive route will mean consistency with the desires of others and can subvert singular rights and self-confidence.

Numerous individuals receive a detached reaction since they have a strong need to be loved by others. Such individuals don't view themselves as equivalents since they place a more noteworthy load on the rights, wishes, and sentiments of others. Detached outcomes have an inability to impart considerations or emotions and results in individuals doing things they truly would not prefer to do, with the expectation that they may please others. This also implies they permit others to assume liability, to lead, and to settle on choices for them.

An exemplary latent reaction is offered by the individuals who state 'yes' to demands when they need to state 'no'.

For instance:

"Do you want to discover an opportunity to wash the vehicle today?"

A run of the mill detached answer may be:

- "Indeed, I'll do it after I've done the shopping, made a significant call, completed the documenting, cleaned the windows, and made lunch for the children!"

An undeniably yet suitable reaction would have been:

- "No, I can't do it today as I have loads of different things I have to do."

The individual reacting truly doesn't have the opportunity, however, their answer doesn't pass on this message. The subsequent reaction is assertive as the individual has considered the ramifications of the solicitation of different errands they need to do.

Assertiveness is significant at work as well as at home.

If you become known as an individual who can't just say no, you will be stacked up with assignments by your partners and directors, and you could even make yourself sick.

At the point when you react like that, you present yourself in a more negative light or put yourself down. If you continually disparage yourself, you will come to feel sub-par compared to other people. While the hidden reasons for detached conduct are regularly poor confidence and esteem, and in itself, it can also lessen sentiments of self-worth, which makes an endless loop.

Being Aggressive
By showing aggression towards someone else, their rights and self-esteem are belittled.

Aggressive conduct neglects to think about the perspectives or sentiments of others. Those acting aggressively will show recognition or energy about others and an aggressive reaction will put others down. Aggressive reactions urge the other individual to react in a non-self-assured way, either aggressively or passively.

There is a wide scope of aggressive practices, including surging somebody superfluously, telling instead of asking, overlooking somebody, or not thinking about another's emotions.

Great relational abilities mean you should know about the various methods for imparting and the distinctive reaction each approach may incite. The utilization of either passive or aggressive conduct in relational connections can have unfortunate ramifications for those you are speaking with and it might well upset making positive head-ways.

It may very well be an alarming or troubling experience to be addressed aggressively and the beneficiary can be left thinking about what of conduct or what the person in question had done to merit the animosity.

If musings and emotions are not expressed plainly, this can prompt people to control others into meeting their desires and wants. Control can be viewed as an undercover type of hostility while amusement can also be utilized aggressively.

Various Situations Call for Different Measures
You may find that you react unexpectedly—regardless of whether passively, self-assuredly, or aggressively—when you are imparting in various circumstances.

Remember that any cooperation is constantly a two-way process and your responses may contrast with your relationship with the other individual in the correspondence.

You may think it's simpler to be assertive to your accomplice than to your chief or vice versa. Nonetheless, regardless of whether it is simple or not, a confident reaction is better for you and your relationship with the other individual.

Why People Are Not Assertive

There are numerous reasons why individuals may act and react in a non-confident way, and this page inspects the most widely recognized ones.

At the point when individuals are not assertive, they can experience the ill effects of lost confidence and self-esteem, which is bound to make them less emphatic later on. It is also imperative to break the cycle and figure out how to be emphatic while regarding the perspectives and assessments of others. As a whole, we reserve a privilege to communicate our emotions, qualities, and feelings.

Low Self-Esteem and Self-Confidence
Sentiments of low self-esteem or self-worth frequently lead to people passively managing others.

By not affirming their privileges, communicating their emotions, or expressing what they need, those with low self-esteem or self-confidence may welcome others to treat them in the same manner. Low self-esteem is fortified in an endless loop of passive reaction and diminished self-confidence.

Jobs
Certain jobs are related to non-assertive conduct like low-status work jobs or the customary job of women. Characteristically, women are viewed as passive while men are relied upon to be aggressive.

There can be an extraordinary weight on individuals to comply with the jobs that are put upon them. You might be more averse to be assertive to your manager at work than you would be to a partner or collaborator who you viewed at an equivalent or lower level than you in the association.

Past Experience
Numerous individuals figured out how to react in a non-confident route through understanding or through displaying their conduct of guardians or other good examples. Scholarly conduct can be hard to unlearn and the assistance of a counselor might be required.

Stress

At the point when individuals are focused, they regularly feel like they have next to zero power over the occasions in their lives.

Individuals who are pushed or on edge can turn to passive or aggressive conduct while communicating their musings and emotions. This will build the sentiments of stress and cause others to feel pushed or on edge too.

See our segment on Stress and Stress Management for additional data on overseeing pressure.

Character Traits
A few people accept they are either passive or aggressive, and at the end of the day, they were brought into the world with specific attributes. There is little they can do to change their type of reaction.

This is usually a wrong assumption since everyone can figure out how to be progressively confident regardless of whether their normal inclinations are passive or aggressive.

Assertiveness Rights and Responsibilities

To be assertive is to comprehend that everybody has fundamental human rights that ought to be regarded and maintained.

Reacting passively can permit such rights to be dismissed or overlooked. Conversely, while acting aggressively, the privileges of others can be manhandled.

Rights that are considered 'individual rights' will change from individual to individual and will vary from culture to culture.

A person's assertive rights ought to include:

- The option to communicate emotions, conclusions, qualities, and convictions.

- The option to adjust one's perspective.

- The option to decide.

- The option to state 'I don't have the foggiest idea' as well as 'I don't comprehend'.

- The option to state 'no' without feeling terrible or regretful.

- The option to be non-emphatic.

- The privilege of individual flexibility, to be one's self.

- The privilege of protection, to be separated from everyone else and be free.

It is also important to adjust the requirements of others against our own. Thought should be offered concern when it is proper to state individual rights and when it isn't.

Recall that the rundown of assertive rights applies to others as well as to yourself. Consequently, every individual should maintain and regard the privileges of others.

Cooperation And Negotiation
Being assertive doesn't imply that individual wishes are naturally allowed: you won't generally get what you need.

Self-assured conduct permits others to state what they need and they may want an alternate result. To conquer a contention, assertiveness requires co-activity and exchange. Co-activity and arrangement permit all gatherings to feel that their perspectives have been perceived and that any choices or results have been reached through common comprehension and exchange.

Managing Non-Assertiveness
Figuring out how to carry on confidently is all well, yet how would you manage non-emphatic conduct in others?

Each connection runs both ways, and figuring out how to manage other people's non-emphatic conduct is a significant ability.

The allurement is to react aggressively or passively to other people's passive or aggressive conduct. This might be a typical situation if they drive you crazy.

This page, nonetheless, discloses how to bargain successfully and confidently with both passive and aggressive conduct.

Managing Passive Behavior
Individuals act passively in light of low self-esteem or confidence. By acting self-assuredly, you should plan to clarify that the other individual's commitments are esteemed and subsequently improves their confidence and self-esteem.

Recollect that it is conceivable to esteem somebody's commitment without essentially concurring with it.

Just as being progressively self-assured ourselves, assertiveness ought to also be empowered in others so they can impart their thoughts and feelings openly without feeling constrained to express certain things.

Assertiveness in others can be supported by utilizing sharpened relational abilities like tuning in, addressing, reflection, and explanation.

A Few Different Ways to Exhibit That You Esteem The Other Individual's Commitment

- Energize their commitment through open addressing, by asking their suppositions, and by attracting individuals into the conversation's circumstances.

- Listen closely to what somebody needs to state before proceeding with the discussion. If important, utilize addressing strategies to explain their feeling before reacting with your own.

- Show that you are keen on what somebody needs to state through proper addressing, reflecting, explanation, and summing up abilities.

- Show that you esteem the other individual's commitment using fitting verbal and non-verbal interchanges like gesturing, grinning, using great eye to eye connection, and empowering language.

- Urge individuals to be open in voicing their emotions, wishes, and thoughts.

- Try not to permit yourself to assume liability for choices that ought to be made together. Rather, bolster others to make their commitment to the conversation.

The more an individual can contribute and feel that their commitment is esteemed, the more they will feel esteemed as a person. The experience of constructive input will assist with expanding an individual's self-confidence. The entire chain of occasions should empower the individual worried to defeat any passive responses and act more confident.

Top Tip!

If you realize that somebody will carry on passively in a conversation or dynamic gathering, at that point you require significant investment to examine their perspectives with them. If you can relate to their feelings and you can help them to express those perspectives in the group.

Dealing With Aggressive Behavior
Taking care of aggressive conduct in others is especially troublesome when it is joined by negative mentalities.

To abstain from reacting protectively or aggressively, self-control is required. It ought to be noticed that aggressive conduct here alludes to verbal and non-verbal messages and not to any type of physical brutality.

Key Techniques That Assists With Managing Aggressive Conduct

- Keep up the self-control. Even though outrage can be a positive power, reacting in an irate way will do little to demoralize animosity. If proper, it'll be set aside to thoroughly consider issues before going into the conversation. It may be useful to state something like, "I need time to consider that", or "Would we be able to discuss this tomorrow when we have additional time?".

- Recall that others reserve an option to their emotions, including outrage. Recognize their resentment by saying "I can see this has truly vexed you, and you're irate about it".

- Stopping, or counting to ten, precedes reacting to upheaval and can assist with abstaining from replying in a programmed, guarded, or aggressive way.

- Attempt to discover territories of concurrence with the other individual, as opposed to concentrating on the differences.

- Discover and show manners by which choices and arrangements can be shared, for example, "How might we discover an answer for this?".

- Attempt to share some empathy with the other individual; how would you feel when you are furious with others?

- It is hard for an individual acting aggressively to quieten down and see things from a more extensive perspective since outrage can be an outflow of individual disappointment.

- Utilizing these strategies should assist you in expressing yourself emphatically instead of aggressively. This should assist with defusing the circumstance and result in positive and successful correspondence.

Assertiveness in Specific Situations: Requests, Criticism, and Compliments
There are three specific circumstances where self-assured conduct is called for, however, it might be especially hard to utilize.

These are the point where you are called up to manage requests, particularly outlandish ones, or criticism, and to offer or get a commendation.

Every one of these circumstances may cause you to feel awkward because you are managing a circumstance where your own and other people's desires might be unrelated. Be that as it may, this is the time where assertiveness is generally significant.

Managing Demands

Managing unsatisfactory requests can be an overwhelming encounter and having the fearlessness to be self-assured in such conditions isn't simple for certain individuals. It should consistently be recognized that everybody has the privilege not to satisfy an interest.

At the point when confronted with interest, thought ought to be given to the accompanying:

- The vast majority are firmly impacted by generalizations, for instance, those of the productive director or the selfless mother. Such speculations can place outlandish requests, desires, and out of line loads upon those holding specific jobs. Everybody has the privilege not to acknowledge the requests related to such jobs.

- While dismissing an interest, clarify that the interest is being dismissed and not the individual.

- Individuals frequently feel that others reserve an option to their time and exertion. You reserve a privilege to state 'no' without legitimizing yourself.

- Having dismissing an interest, it is critical to keep to that choice. If you disintegrate under tension, others will learn how you can be influenced to be so firm. You do reserve the option to alter your perspective if conditions change.

- In setting expectations, individuals frequently resort to passive or manipulative reactions and may also accept a reliance upon the endeavors of others.

Aside from specific exemptions, everybody is answerable for themselves, and undue dependence ought not to be set upon others. Recall that you also have rights!

Assertiveness is discreet and non-aggressive, however, immovably applying those rights, one of which is to reject requests that you consider to be nonsensical, or which you can't meet.

Simultaneously, you also need to perceive the privileges of others to make solicitations of yourself and get a well-mannered reaction.

Managing Criticism
While accepting criticism, set aside some effort to choose whether it is certified criticism, or whether there is some other purpose behind it, for instance, how somebody is irate or baffled, and you are there before them.

Recognize the criticism by rehashing or reflecting it. You may react by saying, "So you feel that I...". Also, with any feedback, it is essential to thank the individual for giving it.

Recognize any honest components of the criticism regardless of whether they are difficult to hear.

If the criticism incorporates a component of truth, attempt to maintain a strategic distance from the normal reaction of lashing back with counter-criticism. Criticism with a trace of truth will be injuring, yet it might be offered with the expectation that it will be utilized well.

With all things considered, not every person is talented in giving feedback.

Assertiveness in Specific Situations: Giving Criticism
If conceivable, abstain from censuring others. Rather, attempt to consider it as 'giving useful, but negative, feedback to change their conduct'. This will assist you with remaining quiet and give feedback more successfully.

Criticism, or contrary feedback, can be tempered to show up less fierce when it is given help by the other individual. Critically, you should guarantee that it is a criticism of the activity as opposed to the individual. Start with a steady remark like, "I welcome all the work you've placed in this, however, we have an issue with..."

Any sentence that starts 'You are' will offend and ought to be maintained a strategic distance away, except if it closes with a commendation. Concentrate on the conduct, not the individual properties of the other person.

Keep any criticism explicit and maintain a strategic distance from all-inclusive statements like, "It was late when you got the children today" as opposed to "No doubt about it". Summed up explanations may not mirror the truth of a circumstance and tend to infer that the individual is to blame when the issue may have been brought about by different troubles or unanticipated conditions.

It is desirable to abstain from accusing another person of causing your emotions, for instance, "You drive me so mad when..." It is smarter to concentrate on yourself as the focal point of your own emotions and, as an option in contrast to the announcement above, you could state "I feel furious when you..."

Assertiveness in Specific Situations: Offering and Receiving Compliments

A few people view the offering and accepting of praises as troublesome or humiliating, and may want to either disregard them or bring them back.

Commending is a constructive method for giving help, indicating endorsement, and expanding the other individual's self-confidence. Figuring out how to both give and acknowledge them effortlessly is a significant fundamental ability.

If a commendation is dismissed, the individual giving it might feel humiliated or limited and may be more averse to give a pat on the back later on.

At the point when you are praised in this way, thank the individual for offering the commendation, and acknowledge it regardless of whether you concur with it. Helpful expressions incorporate "Thank you. That is extremely nice of you to state that", or "Thank you, it was a delight, however, it's constantly ideal to hear that you value it".

When offering a commendation:

- Guarantee it is certified. Unscrupulousness is effectively-identified and will sabotage your endeavors to develop the individual's self-esteem.

- Recollect that encouraging feedback is more successful than a negative fortification. Praises will be recalled more promptly and joyfully than criticism.

- If a commendation isn't fitting, at that point figure out how to state thank you or offer some applause.

Keep in mind, assertiveness is more fitting than a passive or aggressive conduct, regardless of whether it is troublesome. Attempt to regard others as you might want to be dealt with, with deference and amenability. This will assist you in responding confidently to other people, even in troublesome circumstances.

Assertiveness—Tips and Techniques
This section gives some basic hints and strategies that you can use to improve your assertiveness abilities and help other people to communicate in an emphatic manner.

Being decisive can assist us with feeling better about ourselves in developing self-esteem and individual confidence.

How we respond and react to others can cause us to feel deficient, blameworthy, or remorseful. These might be indications of passive conduct. We may also feel furious and disparaging of others during discussions, which might be an indication of aggressive conduct.

This page has a few different ways that both passive and aggressive correspondence can be decreased and supplanted with decisive correspondence, which prompts increasing positive relational collaborations.

While rehearsing these assertiveness strategies, it is imperative to recall what assertiveness is and its significance in the correspondence procedure.

Being confident isn't equivalent to being aggressive; despite what might be expected, assertiveness implies for what you accept.

Assertiveness is communicating your musings, emotions, convictions, and suppositions fairly and suitably. As assertiveness ought to be supported in others it is also critical to recollect that we ought to consistently regard the musings, sentiments, conclusions, and convictions of others.

Assertiveness permits people to affirm their privileges without sabotaging the privileges of others. Assertiveness is viewed as a fair reaction, being neither passive nor aggressive, with self-confidence having a significant impact. A confident individual reacts as an equivalent to other people and plans to be open in communicating their desires, musings, and sentiments.

General Techniques of Assertiveness
Two key methods that can help assertiveness are known as 'Fogging' and the 'Stuck Record' system.

Fogging
Fogging is a valuable method if individuals are acting in a manipulative or aggressive manner.

As opposed to contending back, fogging plans give a negligible, quiet reaction by utilizing terms that are appeasing yet not guarded, while simultaneously not consenting to fulfill needs.

Fogging includes concurring with any reality that might be contained inside articulations regardless of being basic. By not reacting in the normal way and being guarded or factious, the other individual will stop since the ideal impact isn't being accomplished. At the point when the air is less warmed, it will be conceivable to examine the issues more sensibly.

Fogging is named like this because the individual demonstrations like a 'mass of mist' where contentions are tossed, yet not returned.

Model Situation:

"What time do you call this? You're 30 minutes late. I'm tired of you letting me down constantly."

Fogging reaction:

"Indeed, I am later than I wanted to be, and I can see this has irritated you."

"Irritated? I'm irritated because I've been sitting here for a long time. You should attempt to consider other people more."

Fogging reaction:

"Indeed, I was worried that you would be left sitting tight for practically thirty minutes."

"Well...for what reason would you say you were late?"

The Stuck Record Technique
The Stuck Record system utilizes the key confident expertise of 'quiet industriousness'.

It includes rehashing what you need—on numerous occasions—without raising the tone of your voice, losing control, being aggravated, or associated with side issues.

Model Situation:

Envision that you are returning something that is broken to a store. The discussion may go as follows:

"I purchased these shoes a week ago and the heels have crumbled. I want a discount please."

"It would appear that they've been worn a great deal and these shoes were just intended for intermittent wear."

Stuck Record System Reaction:

"I've had them for a week and they're defective. I want a discount please."

"You can't anticipate that I should give you your cash back after you've destroyed them."

Stuck Record Strategy Reaction:

"The heels have tumbled off after a week, and I want a discount please...etc".

Constantly rehashing a solicitation will guarantee the conversation doesn't become diverted with unessential contention. The key is to remain quiet, be extremely clear with what you need, adhere to the point, and don't surrender.

Acknowledge a trade-off only if you're content with the result.

Positive and Negative Inquiry

Positive Inquiry
Positive inquiry is a straightforward strategy for taking care of positive remarks like applause and praises.

Individuals frequently battle with reacting to acclaim and praises, particularly those with lower self-esteem as they may feel deficient, or how the positive remarks are not defended. It is essential to give positive feedback to others when fitting a response suitable to the positive feedback you get.

Positive inquiry is utilized to discover more insights regarding the commendation or recognition given, and concurs with it:

Model Situation
Sender:

"You made an incredible supper today around evening time. It was wonderful!"

Beneficiary:

"Much appreciated. Truly, it was acceptable. What did you specifically like about it?"

This is not quite the same, but as a passive reaction:

"It was no exertion", or "It was only a standard formula".

Negative Inquiry
Something contrary to positive inquiry is negative inquiry. Negative inquiry is an approach to react to progressively negative trades like getting criticism.

Managing criticism can be troublesome, and recollecting any criticism is only someone's sentiment.

Negative inquiry is utilized to discover about basic remarks and is a decent option to progressively aggressive or furious reactions to criticism.

Model Situation
Sender:

"That feast was unpalatable. I can't recall the last time I ate something so horrendous."

Collector:

"It wasn't the best. What didn't you like about it?"

This isn't the same as an aggressive reaction which may have been:

"How could you? I went through the early evening setting up that feast", or "Well, that's the last time I cook for you!"

CHAPTER 4
DEALING WITH BULLIES

Bullying used to be thought of as a kid's playground danger, maybe even as a fundamental transitional experience.

Fortunately, circumstances are different and there is expanding acknowledgment that bullying can influence anybody from adolescence to adulthood, and it makes lives hopeless and unsavory.

Schools and work environments are more mindful of the potential for bullying, and as a rule, they have plans and arrangements set up to oversee it.

The arrangement below discloses how to determine bullying, regardless of whether as the individual being tormented, an associate, parent, or dear companion.

Youthful minds, the psychological well-being noble cause, proposes that over 70% of children have encountered bullying at one time or another.

At the end of the day, regardless of whether you haven't been tormented, you most likely know a considerable amount of individuals who have, or who have seen it. If you're being harassed, you're not the only one.

What is Bullying?

There is no legitimate meanings of bullying.

However, there is a general understanding that bullying is:

Conduct that is intended to hurt another person, or causes them to accomplish something that they would prefer not to do.

This conduct can be either verbal through ridiculing, spreading lies about somebody, or barring them from the gathering, or something physical like kicking and punching somebody.

Verbal or emotional bullying is considerably typical, and it is also harder to spot since menaces will frequently say that it was 'just a joke'. Emotional bullying also leaves no undeniable stamps or wounding, however, in actuality the harm can be significantly more genuine and longer-enduring.

Chitchat Or Bullying?
The issue of chitchat or bullying has entered the standard conversation as of late, with numerous women grumbling that men go excessively far with 'chat', and that they are dependent upon chauvinist, misanthrope insults during evenings out. So when does 'chitchat' become 'bullying'?

There are two different ways to think about the issue.

Initially, is the individual on the less than desirable end okay with the circumstance? This may identify with whether they realize the individuals manage the talk or a 'power irregularity'. For instance, a gathering of companions might be glad with trading sexual jokes about one another. Given that everybody in the gathering is coming in for equivalent consideration, this is presumably okay, if somewhat adolescent. Assuming a similar gathering is concentrating on one individual, and poking sexual fun at that one individual all night, that would presumably be somewhat awkward.

The brilliant standard is:

If they're not happy, at that point it's not chitchat, it's bullying.

The subsequent method to see it is to consider how you would feel if the circumstance was turned on your sibling or sister. For instance, if it's a gathering of men getting some information about the size of her bosoms, would it feel okay if they were stating similar things to a man they didn't know about the size of his penis? Or, on the other hand, if it was your sister on the less than desirable end?

No, most likely not.

That is bullying.

Why Bullying Happens
The purposes behind bullying are self-evident: the bully's objective looks or acts 'in an unexpected way'. For instance, they might be the other gender, an alternate race, an alternate sexual direction, or an alternate size.

On different occasions, there is no undeniable explanation behind that individual being picked as a 'focus', except maybe that they look somewhat powerless.

The reasons why menaces bully are entangled and shifted. They may feel defenseless themselves, and are 'hitting somebody back before they can get hit first'. They might be attempting to get consideration regardless of whether it's from their companions or adults, or they might be irate about something that is occurring in their own lives.

IMPORTANT: Nobody asks to be bullied and no one deserves it.

Also, whatever the issues of the bully are, there is no reason for bullying.

Cyberbullying
Cyberbullying is a new wonder. The term is utilized to portray bullying on the web, frequently employing internet-based life, and for the most part, comprises of unsavory remarks and harsh comments posted openly on the web.

Cyberbullying can also incorporate posting photographs, regardless of whether genuine or photoshopped or making counterfeit records in somebody's name like offering sexual favors.

Cyberbullying is a major issue, and just as harming as 'genuine world' bullying.

Adapting to Bullying General Tips: Tell Someone Else
Regardless of what the domineering jerks state, telling another person will never exacerbate the situation. Tell a trusted companion, parent, or instructor if you are at school. For work environment bullying, talk to a trusted partner, or even gain counsel from your HR group in confidence.

The odds are that you're not by any means the only one being influenced.

Adapting to Bullying General Tips: Request That the Bully Stops
Unhesitatingly and emphatically, reveal to them that you couldn't care less for their conduct, and you would welcome it if they quit calling you names. (or whatever it is.)

The bully may state something like, "Can't you take a joke?", in which case, the appropriate response is something like, "Obviously not, because it's not entertaining".

You should be certain this won't prompt the circumstance to deteriorate, for instance, the bully may get aggressive, yet it's likely worth an attempt.

Adapting to Bullying General Tips: Disregard It and Leave
Menaces need a response. In case you're not annoyed, they'll presumably leave you and locate another unfortunate and unexpecting target.

"I used to be the kind of kid who had sand kicked in his face, presently I'm the kind of kid who watches another person have it kicked in their face."

- Sue Townsend's Adrian Mole

Adapting to Bullying General Tips: Look Confident
Bullying causes individuals to feel little and powerless, which makes them look like simpler targets. If you stroll along with your shoulders down, attempting to get undetectable, it frequently makes you more self-evident.

Instead, set your shoulders back, raise your head, and step out. You'll look more sure, and to a lesser degree, an objective.

Point by point guidance is also accessible from hostile to bullying causes and sites, for example, like Bullying UK and Young Minds.

Childline (0800 1111) is also accessible in the UK if you wish to talk in confidence to somebody.

No-one Should be bullied. No one requests to be harassed, and no one ought to need to endure it.

Adapting to Bullying General Tips: Confronting Bullying
We all concur that bullying is horrendous and pointless, and how it should never occur.

In some way or another, when we see bullying transpiring somewhere else, we might be hesitant to intercept due to the paranoid fear of pushing ourselves into difficulty or maybe compounding the situation.

This section gives some exhortation as to how and when to get involved when another person is being harassed, and how you can help without exacerbating the situation.

A Philosophical Thought
"The only thing necessary for the triumph of evil is for good men to do nothing." - John Stuart Mill
If you acknowledge John Stuart Mill 's words, at that point we should confront bullying when we see it.

So, for what reason is it so difficult to mediate? You might be thinking:

- Consider the possibility that the bully may aggravate it.

- Consider the possibility that the bully turns on me next.

All of these are possible. In any case, despite everything, that doesn't excuse you of the need to get involved and attempt to help one way or another.

Helping Someone You Know Who is Being Bullied

If you see somebody you know being tormented, maybe a companion, child, or partner, you have a few alternatives:

- Contingent upon your degree of confidence, you might have the option to intervene straight away and saying something like, "I don't believe that's a worthy method to converse with anybody. Might you want to reevaluate how you said that?" This is probably going to work better with adults, who may well not be aware of how they are talking or how it is probably going to be seen.

- You might have the option to converse with the bully later and reveal to them that you thought their conduct was faulty. Once more, this is probably going to work better with adults who might be unaware of how their conduct could be deciphered, yet there is no motivation to assume it would not work with more youthful individuals.

- You can converse with the individual being tormented later to check whether they are okay and offer to help them, for instance, going with them to tell another person and collaborate their story as an observer. Simply having somebody address them might be sufficient to convince them that they should tell another person. This is always a positive advance.

- You can include them in your gathering and make them less of a target and assist with guaranteeing that they're not taken off alone where the bully can discover them.

- You can mention to a confided adult or associate about what is happening in confidence. If the individual concerned is an adult, you can address the HR division in your work environment and approach them for counsel. As a child, you can address your parents, an instructor, or a youth laborer.

Confronting Bullying in Public
If the bullying is occurring out in the open, the best activity required is to ask whether they are okay, or if they need you to help. You would then be able to choose what move to make.

Top Tip!

If you're worried about drawing attention to yourself, go up to the individual and state, "Hello. I haven't seen you for a long time! How are you?" Also give them an embrace. While you are doing this, you can ask them unobtrusively, and without causing anyone to notice, "Is it accurate to say that you are okay, or would you like some assistance?"

They would then be able to state, "I'm fine", or "Yes please", or even "Gracious, it's so acceptable to see you. We should leave and get up to speed someplace quieter."

If you don't mind note that this is a lot simpler for a woman to do to with another woman. For a man to do this to a lady may look somewhat undermining, regardless of whether she was in a difficult situation. Rather, it's better just to state, unobtrusively, "You look somewhat awkward. Is everything okay?"

Confronting Your Friends
If you're a piece of the gathering, raising hell, and you begin to feel somewhat awkward with the degree of 'talk' going on, you can either:

- Confront the others and propose it's most likely gone too far (the odds are that others in the gathering will also think in this way, and will assist you with moving on); or

- Attempt interruption: present another subject of discussion and check whether you can dismiss the gathering. Once more and almost certainly, others will invite this and bolster your turn. For instance, you may state, "Now look, please, we said we would grab a bite. Where will we go?"

The second option is probably going to work better if the gathering is somewhat drunk. You can, and most likely should, have the main discussion at some other point, when everybody is calm and can perceive any reason as to why there may have been an issue.

Confronting Cyberbullying
It is also essential to confront cyberbullying, or bullying on the web.

Once more, this might involve confronting individuals that you see as companions. The appropriate response might be to adopt a comedic strategy.

For instance, if you hear a remark which looks exceptionally unfavorable, include another that says something like:

"Ouch! I don't assume you implied it like that? Do you understand how bad that sounded?"

This will give the other individual the alternative of saying sorry and include that they didn't mean it in that way. If you don't feel ready to do that, you can report the substance to the site concerned, and request that they explore and expel the culpable remark or post.

Taking the Hard Road

It is never going to be anything but difficult to confront and challenge bullying when you see it occurring.

It is imperative to do, both for yourself and those included.

It is also worth considering that it's difficult to challenge bullying, but it's interminably harder to be forced to bear it.

Helping Someone Else Cope with Bullying

This page gives point by point and explicit guidance about what to do if you are the subject of bullying, including who to tell and what may occur straight away.

While a great part of the data on this page may also be pertinent to work environment bullying, you may also prefer to peruse our explicit page on Bullying in the Workplace.

You Are Not Alone

As a matter of first importance, it might feel if you are being harassed and that you're not the only one.

A few assessments recommend that up to 70% of children have encountered bullying sooner or later, even though this incorporates as a culprit, casualty, and witness.

Bullying is a major issue across societies and age-groups. There is help accessible and things will show signs of improvement.

The subsequent thought to recall is that it isn't your fault.

Whatever you think, no matter how low your confidence or self-esteem is, you have to recall that bullying isn't your fault. However, you must address it.

Tending to Bullying

There are four primary strides in overseeing bullying:

1. Tell Someone Else.

2. Request That The Bully Stop.

3. Overlook It and Walk Away.

4. Look Confident.

1. Tell Someone Else
You may not be distant from everyone else but you do need to mention to somebody what's going on.

You are probably not going to have the option to determine the bullying yourself, or you would have done that already.

Who you tell may rely upon who is bullying you and where. While it is basic for menaces to be known to their casualties through school, this isn't the main alternative. For instance, children at one school might be harassed and head to class with at least one child from another nearby school.

You could tell:

A friend as the same age as you or an older one, who may have more understanding and could exhort you. A few schools run 'pal' plans, so you may decide to ask your 'friend' for exhortation.

Your folks, who will more than likely not need to know that eventually. It might be simpler to reveal that to them yourself, and sooner as opposed to sitting tight for them to discover from another person or educator.

It is significant!

If the bullying proceeds after a move has been made to stop it, continue telling individuals it is occurring. If you don't continue letting them know, they won't know it despite everything that is happening.

If you are being harassed through the web (cyberbullying), either via web-based networking media like Facebook, you can utilize the CEOP button (Child Exploitation and Online Protection Center) to report it.

If the bully is at your school, the school ought to have an enemy of the bullying arrangement, which it should follow. This implies sanctions against a bully like a break from the study hall or even prohibition.

2. Request That The Bully Stops
This subsequent advance might be troublesome, particularly if you have permitted the bullying to continue for a long while before telling anyone else.

You may be asked by the school to have a gathering with the bully:

- If you would prefer not to do this, you don't need to do this. Consider how it might have a positive impact.

- The bully might be unconscious of how terrible you feel, and it might bring them up short (this is the standard behind casualty sway explanations in court).

- Work on keeping your conveyance sure and confident, and clarify that you don't care for their conduct, and you would value it if they halted.

3. Overlook It and Walk Away

No one is proposing that you ought to endure bullying. It is disagreeable and unsatisfactory.

Be that as it may, menaces frequently state or do things since they need a response from their casualty. In case you're not troubled by what they state or do, they may well disregard you and locate a new compensating objective.

Shockingly, they may also raise their activities in the desire for getting a response.

It is essential to comprehend that occasionally, the most secure method for overseeing some else's conduct is to be somewhere else.

4. Look Confident
No one requests to be tormented. However, a few people may look like simple targets because they look somewhat defenseless.

Research shows that individuals who walk and stand in confidence are considerably less liable to be assaulted. If you are feeling somewhat defenseless, ensure that you stand upright, set your shoulders back, and step out. This will have two impacts:

- It will make you look certain, which will make you more averse to turn into a casualty of bullying or some other assault; and

- It will, strangely, cause you to feel certain. The body reflects the psyche, however, the brain is also influenced by the body.

What Happens Next?
With karma and great care taken by your school and by you, these activities should end the bullying.

If all else fails and if the bullying doesn't stop, and it is affecting your instruction or making you hopeless, you might have the option to change schools. This is an interesting point in the more extended term, and examine this with your parents.

Point by point guidance is also accessible from being hostile to bullying sites, for example, Bullying UK and Young Minds.

A Problem Shared...

An issue shared may not exactly be an issue divided, yet taking a step to converse with somebody about bullying is the initial move towards settling the circumstance.

As opposed to what bullies will regularly attempt to state, detailing them won't exacerbate things. Schools and work environments don't, and ought not, endure bullying. Make it simpler for them to deal with the circumstance and stamp out bullying by announcing it at whatever point and at any place it occurs.

Helping Someone to Cope with Bullying

It tends to be terrible as a parent to see your child being tormented and not realize what to do to support them. This page gives counsel about helping them to build up the aptitudes to challenge and forestall bullying, and how to help them report and deal with the issue if it happens.

Although this page centers around youth, bullying is a significant part of the data that is applicable to adults who are being tormented.

Forestalling Bullying

There is no motivation behind why somebody is picked as an objective for bullying. It is frequently obvious that the individuals who seem helpless are bound to become targets.

It is along these lines to show children's assertiveness.

It might also be useful to work on bullying avoidance practices like leaving or trying to avoid panicking under pressure.

Careful discipline brings about promising results, so it is a smart thought to talk about and practice these as a major aspect of your child's turn of events.

Specifically:

- Urge your child to 'walk tall', putting their head up, and bear their back, and stride out with confidence.

- Help your child to create self-confidence and flexibility.

- Talk about undermining circumstances, and how to keep away from them, for instance, by utilizing another course.

- Try not to endure aggressive or upsetting conduct in your child or any deprecatory comments about others. Clarify why this sort of conduct or language isn't satisfactory, and that it makes others miserable, regardless of whether it was implied as a joke.

- Show your child systems (like the 'Trashcan' Technique) to assist them with discarding any divergence focused on them.

The 'Trashcan' Technique

This system, utilized by a child's power to battle bullying, is a solid representation method. At the point when somebody says something horrendous to you, envision botching the words into a little ball and tossing them in the canister. At that point supplant them with something positive.

For instance:

If somebody says "You're moronic", you can discard that, and supplant it with "I know I'm canny".

If somebody says "I'm not your companion any longer", you can supplant it with "I will discover different companions".

This is a minor departure from Neuro-Linguistic Programming and is extremely ground-breaking.

Show your child compelling social abilities to assist them with maintaining a strategic distance of avoidance from the gathering. For instance, tell them the best way to request and participate in the gathering.

Ensure that your child realizes that physical activity like hitting or kicking is unsuitable. A self-safeguard class may assist them with understanding the contrast between hostility and resistance, and tell them the best way to shield themselves without being aggressive. This will help both in managing bullying and in keeping your child from being viewed as a bully.

Identifying Bullying
Children and adults are regularly hesitant to concede that they are being tormented. This is because they feel that telling will exacerbate

things, and at times it is because they believe that it is in one way or another their deficiency.

The primary concern: nobody asks or has the right to be harassed.

You can tell that somebody is being harassed due to specific signs:

- Their conduct may change, and they may turn out to be considerably more pulled back and uncommunicative;

- They may go out less because they are being avoided by the gathering;

- They may appear to have less cash since it is being taken;

- They may turn out to be exceptionally on edge when they get a book or email message if it is upsetting;

- They may get stressed over going to class, and even play truant. This may also show itself in migraines or different indications of sickness on school days. they may begin to get along nicely at school.

There are numerous things other than bullying which can also make children become stressed and show comparable practices.

It's a given that you ought to consistently urge your children to converse with you about anything that is annoying them. It might be useful to make additional changes to talk, maybe by doing things together like strolling or cooking.

You can even say, "You appear to be extremely tranquil. Is anything disturbing you?", or "I've seen...Is there something occurring?"

If it is an associate, you may make a chance to talk like getting together and inquiring whether everything is okay.

When you know about the issue, you would then be able to assist them with managing it.

Helping Someone to Cope With Bullying
If somebody discloses to you that they're being harassed, it is imperative to listen cautiously without judgment or an emotional reaction. Use inquiries to explain, but be mindful not to utilize 'driving inquiries'.

Know about your own emotions, maybe as a result of your earlier encounters in life. These will influence how you react and it could be unhelpful. Ensure that you apply rationale and objective speculation to the circumstance as well as emotion.

Console the individual included that it isn't their fault.

Ask them how they might want to take it forward, and what they may want from you. Would they, for instance, want you to accompany them to converse with somebody about it?

Support a presentation of self-confidence by telling them the best way to stand and walk away. Also, energize an absence of response to the bullying, while at the same time clarifying this isn't tied in with enduring it, it's tied in with indicating that you couldn't care less, so the bully surrenders.

Urge them to grow new aptitudes or interests, to give them another outlet and something else to consider.

NEVER:

- Advise anybody to hit the bully, or call them names as well;

- Excuse the experience. Continuously talk about it delicately, and help them to consider how to adapt, regardless of whether you don't feel that it's 'truly' bullying.

- When or if you concur, the school/HR/supervisors ought to be involved:

- Help them to record a course of events of what has occurred. Guarantee that they are as explicit since this will support any examination;

- Arrange to see somebody, don't simply turn up. This may be a Human Resources proficient, your child's instructor, a peaceful consideration educator, or head of the school. Your child may have solid perspectives about who they might want you to see, so set yourself to be adaptable;

- Make it understood in conversations that you might want to work with the school or working environment to discover an answer. It is significant that they don't get guarded, and that you don't blame them for anything;

- Recollect that it will require some investment to discover what occurred. Ask when you may get notifications from them, or orchestrate a subsequent gathering to talk about things further.

- Ensure they keep on tracking any further episodes (counting date, time, what occurred, and any observers), and give this to the individual managing it. It might also be useful to track their reaction.

Your Child Being The Bully

You trust that your very much raised little angel would not fantasize about bullying anybody. Yet, menaces have guardians as well.

If your child is blamed for bullying, you have to pay attention to the allegation very closely.

This DOES NOT mean surging down to the school (or the other child's folks) to confront them and blame them for lying.

Rather, it implies listening discreetly and normally to what is being stated and concentrating on the proof. You should approach your child with their side of the story.

Be readied to consider that your child might be deceiving you, particularly if the proof is clear.

You should work with the school to build up an answer. The school will presumably need to force approvals, and you may also wish to force your own at home.

A Final Thought...

Bullying consistently summons forceful emotions, frequently connected to individual encounters. At the point when you are helping somebody to adapt to bullying, or oversee bullying, know about your emotional reactions as they may cloud your capacity to offer reasonable counsel.

CHAPTER 5
ACHIEVING RESILIENCE

Resilience is the 'elastic ball' factor: the capacity to bounce back in case of misfortune or adversity.

Set forth plainly, resilience is the capacity to cope and adapt to the situation, issues, and set-backs you meet throughout your life and return more grounded from them.

Resilience depends on various aptitudes and draws on different wellsprings of help, including sane reasoning abilities, physical and emotional wellness, and your associations with people around you.

Resilience isn't really about beating enormous difficulties; every single one of us faces a lot of difficulties where we should draw on our stores of resilience.

Four Ingredients of Resilience

There are four essential fixings to resilience:

- Mindfulness – seeing what is happening around you and inside your head;

- Thinking – having the option to decipher the occasions that are going on soundly;

- Connecting – how we call upon others to assist us with meeting the difficulties that we face since resilience is about realizing when to request help; and

- Fitness – our psychological and physical capacity to adapt to the difficulties without getting sick.

The Link Between Thought and Emotion
How you think can be influenced by your emotional reaction to the circumstance, and part of staying alert is understanding this and remembering when it occurs.

Psychologist Albert Ellis made a straightforward model for this, which he called A-B-C for Adversity – Beliefs – Consequences. This model sets out a procedure.

As our page on Managing Emotions clarifies, in some cases, an emotion is instinctive to the point that there is no opportunity to experience this procedure normally: you respond quickly to the circumstance by fleeing or shouting. Yet, your brain has more likely than not experienced the procedure subliminally.

It is also critical to perceive that specific contemplations lead to specific emotions.

The model includes:

- I've lost something: Sadness

- Somebody has planned something to hurt me: Anger

- I've harmed somebody: Shame

- I feel undermined by something: Fear

The advantage of understanding that these considerations lead to specific emotions is by distinguishing the emotion we believe, and what we can comprehend by what our inner mind perspectives might be. This may not be evident in something else, and it will assist us in taking the correct activity to address the issue.

Thinking Traps
Purported 'believing traps' will be traps into which we can fall in our deduction, as a rule at the 'B' phase of the A-B-C model above.

Thinking traps are adequately suppositions about ourselves or the circumstance, made without inspecting the proof, and are generally unhelpful.

The signs that you are tending are categorized as one of the reasoning snares that incorporate the utilization of expressions like 'never', 'consistently', and 'I...they...', for instance:

"I can't do maths", "I've always been unable to do things like that", "They've removed it from me".

In case you're believing that this language sounds extremely silly, you should be aware of falling into one of these reasoning snares when you are building up your convictions about a circumstance since it could keep you from acting successfully: as it were, figuring traps can keep you from acting with resilience.

Improving Resilience Through Thinking
Having thought about the components of resilience, and the way toward reacting to circumstances, it might now be useful to discuss what we can do to help create flexibility.

There are a lot of helpful techniques here, including:

1. Assembling More Information

You need to draw in the discerning piece of your brain in your decision-making about the circumstance.

Perhaps the most ideal approach to do so is to effectively accumulate more information on which to base your choice on.

Assume that you see a snake by your side. Your prompt response may be dread:

"A snake! It must be harmful! I would do well to flee!" [A-B-C]

However, take a brief reprieve and accumulate more information. It may be dead. It probably won't be harmful. It may be cold, and along these lines just equipped for moving gradually.

There is a wide range of reasons why you shouldn't have to flee.

A pivotal part of social interaction is to consider elective clarifications for the circumstance.

Your mind, given your experience and your conviction framework, will give you what it considers to be the clearest clarification.

Be that as it may, it may not be right!

Contemplating options, and checking those against the real world, maybe by posing inquiries of others or looking into something, will assist with guaranteeing that you respond properly to the circumstance.

2. Alternative Scenarios

We're all inclined to envisioning the most terrible conclusion.

Your manager requests to address you, and you promptly envision that you're going to be terminated. You prepare to protect your ongoing performance, yet when you enter her office—things being what they are—she needs you to realize that she's pregnant and you're in line to assume control over her obligations while she's on maternity leave, with an ensuing compensation rise.

Your child's educator requests a fast word after school. You quickly accept that the child is in a tough situation, yet no, they simply fell and cut their knee at noon. No mischief was done, but the school needs to tell you.

Envisioning the most noticeably awful situation is also called catastrophizing, and it is shockingly normal.

There is a simple approach to manage it, which includes producing elective situations in your mind:

Envision the most terrible situation and let your creative mind go crazy. What could have turned out so badly? What may have occurred?

Presently consider the most ideal results. How great would it be?

At long last, consider the most probable results—likely somewhere close to the two. Arrange how you will react to that.

These two methodologies, assembling more information, and searching for elective situations, will assist you with developing your resilience.

You will turn out to be more mindful of what is happening around you and inside your head (mindfulness). They will also assist you with applying levelheaded deduction to the circumstance, moving out of any speculation traps into which you have fallen, and understanding and excusing your emotional reaction to a circumstance.

Improving Resilience Through Reaching Out
"No man is an island, entire of itself; every man is a piece of the continent." - John Donne (English Poet)

There is no shame in requesting help. We need assistance every once in a while, and a significant number of us work much better when we are working with others.

A decent piece of versatility is realizing when and how to approach others for help, contacting those who we have connections with, and to determine to gain help with our issues.

Improving Fitness and Health
The last component of resilience is physical and psychological wellness.

Become familiar with emotional insight and how to successfully oversee individual connections at home, busy working, and with social interaction.

Flexibility is a multi-faceted capacity. To confront difficulties and react properly, it can expect us to draw on the entirety of our assets, both inside and outside, including our connections.

Fortunately improving our assets can assist with creating resilience, and there are numerous manners by which we can do that.

7 Pillars of Resilience to Master Any Challenge

Numerous individuals wonder how to get more grounded as far as professional and private success is concerned. What are the best devices to assist you with leaving your usual range of familiarity and avoid it for something other than a minor second? What are the procedures that set us up to deal with pressure, extended hours, and peak performance without undesirable side effects like burnout?

I encountered these difficulties myself when I first began self-imposed objectives like 'How to Travel the World for Free'. Friends of mine had something to say about it. The inquiry emerged concerning how I prepared my flexibility to adapt to such extreme travel without a penny in my pocket. My answer was quite clear 'I simply don't have a clue'.

I thought about this inquiry and understood that I probably tested my resilience during the earlier experience in life and have become a strong individual.

Furthermore, by thinking back I understood that I wasn't versatile ten or fifteen years sooner. Things being what they are, what was the deal? Also, how might you ensure you become as versatile as conceivable to deal with pressure and difficulties with confidence and quality?

I love this Huffington Post article on resilience:

'Versatility. Making chicken plate of mixed greens out of chicken crap. Partying like there's no tomorrow despite learning about consume blue', and 'There's excellence in versatility...There's mental fortitude in flexibility...There's solace in resilience...'

Resilient individuals are practically happy individuals who master the craft of existence. I can express this since I used to be an individual who would search for issues and not arrangements. I can even depict the youthful immature me as skeptical at certain stages. What's more, I'm happy I have understood that these psychological stages will keep you away from making progress and bliss.

How about we take a look at the supposed seven mainstays of resilience?

- Reasonable Optimism

- Acknowledgment

- Solution Orientation

- Self-Regulation

- Assuming Responsibility

- Network Orientation

- Future Planning

I ask anybody perusing this article to scale every one of the seven mainstays of resilience from zero to ten. Zero signifies 'not great in' and ten signifies 'got everything'. At that point please include all your numbers together.

I would consider anybody accomplishing more than fourty-five points as an entirely strong individual, yet anybody beneath fifty-five points can truly profit by taking a shot at their flexibility. Just to tell you, my score was around only thirty-five around fifteen years ago. These days I believe my score to be fifty or above. What's more, it feels great to experience existence with these seven columns!

1. Reasonable Optimism
Reasonable optimism encourages us to maintain a strategic distance from superfluous feelings of dread and self-forced obstructions that keep us away from our accomplishing objectives. If we look at challenges with the mentality of 'that won't work', we will dread the outcomes and probably won't attempt to begin accomplishing them.

On the opposite side, an unreasonable optimism can conceivably lead us to hazardous conduct and undesirable results. That is the reason sensible, good faith is the best way to turn into an achiever.

There are a few ways to abandon a worrier to a hopeful person.

Chipping away at your center convictions is an effective instructing apparatus to help us change our minds.

I might want to encourage everybody to keep a journal recording the idea of their contemplations as the day progresses. This assists with distinguishing negative considerations and projections, which empowers you to transform them into positive ones. Reflection can bolster this procedure as well.

2. Acknowledgment of The Unchangeable
Some circumstances may trouble us, yet we need to acknowledge that we don't have any reasonable possibility of evolving them. Going on about them, for example, 'For what reason is the climate so terrible once more', just keeps us in an unsatisfied state. The same goes for the absence of daylight, the absence of well-disposed drivers in

urban areas, or the undesirable responses of certain people. We can help ourselves by tolerating these conditions as unchangeable!

3. Solution Orientation

As referenced before, solution orientation is a decision. Would I like to go on about the issue and burn through my time, or would I like to take a look at solutions and proceed onward?

4. Self-Regulation

This column contains the capacities of self-inspiration, overseeing pressure, self-order, and self-control.

We have the decision to reinforce this pillar as far as objective setting, limit setting, and responsibility to ourselves. I improved my self-inspiration by contriving a lot of present moment and long-haul objectives, and it has completely changed me. An existence without objectives effectively will become dull. Don't hesitate to look at persuasive motivation on my inspirational courses site.

5. Assuming Responsibility

We may all have just fallen into the 'it's-his-shortcoming trap'.

Fundamentally, this is a side effect without the fourth pillar of resilience. Self-responsibility is a significant part of escaping an emergency because self-responsibility empowers us to acknowledge wrongdoings and discover snappy activities for arrangements. The 'it's-his-shortcoming trap' keeps us in an unreliable state absent with a lot of activity.

Don't hesitate to add this activity to your journal and note when the snare hits you. No concerns, we're not all great. Simply note the circumstances in your everyday convention and figure out how to grasp change.

6. Network Orientation
Network orientation is significant in empowering you to find support in an emergency. It merits asking oneself, 'How great is my social encouraging group of people'?

If you need more companions or partners, it's totally fine. Dejection is one of the primary instigators of sorrow. There's consistently time to improve your system. Another significant part of the fifth pillar is the capacity to connect with others and request help by conceding that there may be an emergency. Character attributes like pride (regular in men) can be deterrents that are valuable to survive. System direction emphatically encourages you, both secretly and expertly, to discover arrangements that can't be found all alone.

7.Future Planning
As referenced previously, the objective setting can be the cure to an absence of inspiration and even sadness. I use the objective setting and future arranging as a significant device with my customers to conquer despondency. Things that come causes us to have a need to live, defeat hindrances, and look forward not in reverse.

In conclusion, resilience is something other than a blend of perspectives to carry on with a more joyful life. Resilience is the intensity of 'making chicken serving of mixed greens out of chicken poo'.

Resilience work hasn't just recently empowered me to confront adventure difficulties, it has also helped me to relocate to the US and start a satisfying inspirational business by failing to look back or letting apprehension and cynicism deal with the progressions I made. If you take a shot at resilience, the result will be a lot more noteworthy than you anticipate at present. Appreciate this unfathomable way of inspiration and power!

CHAPTER 6

POSITIVE THINKING

Positive thinking is the possibility that you can completely change yourself by thinking positively about things.

This thought can sound somewhat delicate and cushy, which is something of an issue for some individuals who perceive that simply thinking about great contemplations won't change the world and dispose of the entire thought.

In any case, research shows that positive thinking truly has a logical premise. You can't change the world, yet you can change how you see it and respond to it. Also, that can change the way how you feel about yourself as well as other people, which can hugely affect your well-being.

Quick Tips to Enable Positive Thinking

- Deal With Yourself: Do not be incredulous of yourself to other people. While it very well may be valuable to trust your interests to somebody you trust, telling the world is something different. Be benevolent to yourself. Make a rundown of your great characteristics and trust them. Have confidence in yourself.

- Try Not To Be A Complainer: By being negative you can confine yourself from others and cut yourself off from positive answers for issues.

- Figure Out How To Relax: Allow time for yourself every day, only for a couple of moments. It is critical to discover time to unwind and loosen up.

- Lift Your Morale: Treat yourself every once in a while, particularly if you have beaten an issue or made an individual accomplishment.

- Never Forget: Praise yourself on a vocation/task well done and perhaps tell a companion. Supported applause is a decent lift to confidence.

- Figure Out How To Channel Nerves and Tension Positively: When you are anxious, adrenaline is siphoned through the body and you feel keyed up and alert. This additional vitality can be utilized to acceptable impact; empowering you to speak with more prominent energy and force.

- Figure Out How To Be Assertive: Stand up for what you put stock in and don't be forced by others. See our segment on assertiveness for more information.

The Effect of Negative Thinking

To comprehend the impact of positive thinking, it's useful to consider negative thinking first.

Most negative emotions like dread or outrage, are intended to help with endurance. They cause us to make quick and powerful moves to spare ourselves from whatever is compromising us. This implies they also keep us from being diverted by different things around us.

Negative thinking isn't so extraordinary in present-day settings. If you have a great deal to do, and you're stressed that you won't complete everything, the exact opposite thing you need is for your mind to close down and concentrate just on what extent your schedule is.

Negative thinking is a propensity, something you can prepare your mind to keep away from. Steady negative thinking can make you substantially more liable to be pushed and can prompt significant issues such as wretchedness.

The Power of Positive Thinking

Barbara Fredrickson, a specialist at the University of North Carolina, did a great investigation with five groups of individuals where she indicated each group images intended to incite an alternate emotional reaction.

- Group 1 saw images intended to trigger sentiments of happiness;

- Group 2's images were chosen to cause them to feel mollified;

- Group 3's images were nonpartisan;

- Group 4 saw images to make them apprehensive; and

- Group 5 saw a progression of images intended to drive them mad.

Each group was then approached to record what moves they would make in a circumstance that made comparative sentiments.

Groups 4 and 5 recorded less activities than different groups. Groups 1 and 2 recorded the most activities.

As such, feeling positive emotions causes you to distinguish more prospects and choices throughout your life.

In any case, it may be fascinating that these additional prospects and choices appear to convert without hesitation.

Individuals who think more positively are bound to get things done based on those choices. They assemble new abilities and create existing ones, with the goal that they truly have more alternatives throughout everyday life.

Positive Thinking in Practice

Top-notch preliminaries for new drugs and treatments think about a treatment group, which gets the new treatment, with a 'control group' that doesn't.

In any case, when in doubt, these benchmark groups don't simply have 'no treatment'. Rather, they get a 'fake treatment', that is, a treatment substitute which seems as though it's the genuine article, yet it has no physical impact. Instances of fake treatments incorporate sugar pills or seasoned water rather than authentic tablets or medications.

For what reason do they get a fake treatment? As a result of the intensity of positive thinking...

The 'Misleading Effect' is a well-reported marvel in medication, where individuals imagine that they are being given a powerful treatment are bound to recuperate than the individuals who realize that their treatment is the same old thing.

The misleading impact may sound remarkable, yet it has been seen over and over in clinical preliminaries.

The exercises are twofold:

New medicines need to 'beat' fake treatments to be certain that they have a genuine impact; and

The brain is a very useful asset and, assuming there is any chance of this happening, human services specialists should assist their patients with drawing on it.

A positive demeanor will likely not fix malignant growth in itself. Be that as it may, positive thinking will make it simpler to deal with your life, lessen pressure, and help you to deal with yourself better. Also, those things are critical to assist you with recouping from genuine ailments. *Caution! Try not to force it!*

Positive thinking is acceptable. In any case, you ought to do whatever it takes not to utilize it to shut out everything negative that occurs in your life. Every now and then awful stuff occurs, and you will feel down about it. It's horrible imagining that you don't because constrained positive thinking can be counterproductive.

What you have to stay away from is the 'creating debacle' situation. (the 'my life is an all-out fiasco' tape that plays in your mind.) The most ideal approach to do that isn't to disclose to yourself that your life is great. Rather, you have to perceive what has turned out badly, however, set it in the setting.

For instance:

"Truly, I'm having an awful day, however, tomorrow will be better. I will return home now and I will have the option to think about an answer for the issue toward the beginning of the day when I am less worn out."

Tamar Chamsky, a clinical psychologist, calls this 'Conceivable Thinking', and research proposes that it is the most ideal approach to recuperate from troublesome occasions.

Developing Habits of Positive Thinking

If you consider positive reasoning 'being upbeat', it is a lot simpler to work out what you ought to do to create propensities dependent on it.

For instance, what do you like doing?

Research shows that there are three excellent approaches to manufacture positive reasoning aptitudes:

1. Meditation
Individuals who contemplate each day show more positive intuition than the individuals who don't.

Is that the meditation causing the positive reasoning, or simply having the opportunity to think? It's difficult to tell, but on the other hand, it's difficult to contend with science. Individuals who reflect will show more care or capacity to embrace the here and now, which is also connected with positive reasoning.

2. Composing
A gathering of students had gotten some information about a seriously positive encounter each day for three days in a row.

Incredibly, they would be wise to mention their state of mind and better physical well-being thereafter, and the impact went on for a significant long time. This is a truly simple activity: you could, for instance, compose a blog concentrating on positive encounters or keep a journal.

3. Play
It's essential to set aside a few minutes for yourself to have some good times.

You may need to place it into your journal to constrain yourself to make time, regardless of whether it's to meet a companion for espresso or go out for a walk/bicycle ride.

The Skills You Need Guide to Life: Looking After Yourself
In light of our most well-known substance, this book will assist you with living a more joyful, more beneficial, and increasingly profitable life.

Figure out how to look after your body and mind by being aware of the central initial steps to self-awareness.

A Virtuous Circle
Happy individuals—those with a positive point of view—are more joyful, yet also appear to accomplish more.

While achievement may prompt bliss, there is almost no inquiry that joy prompts achievement.

Seeing time as a positive thing about your life, you do the things that cause you to feel positive emotions like bliss. It is imperative to helping you to create aptitudes and develop as an individual.

CHAPTER 7

HOW TO BUILD CONFIDENCE THROUGH MEDITATION

Confidence is a faith in yourself and your capacities.

It causes you to feel great about yourself, and it permits you to perform better at any movement.

At the point when you're sure you can converse with anybody about anything, And you can play sports at a more significant level. Also, you can accomplish more gainful and inventive work.

In this chapter, I'll mention why meditation is a very effective approach to construct confidence. And afterward, I'll give you three simple strides to learn meditation to begin today.

Advantages of Meditation (for Confidence)

There are innumerable medical advantages to meditation (all demonstrated in logical examinations):

- Upgraded Immune System

- Reduced Blood Pressure

- Improved Digestion

However, the number one reason meditation grows confidence is that it stops negative self-talk!

Meditation prepares your brain to separate itself from the steady 'mental babble' going on inside your head. What's more, this 'psychological prattle' is the thing that makes you lose confidence and get restless in any case!

At the end of the day, meditation permits you to understand that you don't need to tune in to the voice inside your head, particularly when it's being negative and concentrating on 'terrible' things about yourself. (for example what you look like, people's opinion of you, and so forth.)

Consider it along these lines: when you're feeling certain it's quite often joined by a total absence of reasoning. You're in the zone. You don't think, you simply DO!

At the point when you're feeling restless or unreliable, it's quite often joined by a lot of reasoning...and it's normally self-damaging contemplating how you're going to screw things up.

By contemplating routinely, it gets simpler to 'get in the zone,' turn your mind off, and stop negative self-talk. This is the reason examiners have discovered that meditation 'expands social self-confidence, friendliness, general mental well-being, and social development'. Different investigations have performed MRI outputs and found that contemplating can build the convergence of dim issues in zones of your brain related to managing emotions, thoughtfulness, and empathy while diminishing dim issues in districts of the mind related to nervousness, dread, and stress. Set forth plainly: reflecting can truly modify your brain to be not so much on edge, but rather more certain!

Now, how about we talk about three simple steps you can use to build confidence in meditation...

Step #1: Learn How to Meditate

How about we make one thing straight: there is no 'right' approach to think.

That being stated, an essential care meditation is most likely best since it is so natural to get. More or less, care meditation rotates around being 'careful'. (for example, concentrating on the physical vibes of the current second.)

The most straightforward approach to do this is to concentrate on your relaxing. This works since when you center completely around every inward breath and every exhalation, it's extremely hard to consider anything else.

Here is a brisk and simple approach to incorporate this:

- Take a seat on the floor or in a chair. (maintain a tall, erect stance.)

- Set a brief clock on your telephone.

- Start breathing through your nose.

- Feel the cool air enter your nose (and your midsection ascend) with every inward breath.

- Feel the warm air leave your nose (and let your body unwind) with every exhalation.

- That is truly everything necessary. At the point when you find yourself considering anything but your breathing (and you certainly will), essentially re-center around the following inward breath.

Step #2: Build The Habit of Meditating

Meditation isn't something that you can do only a single time or twice, and in a split second receive the entirety of the rewards.

In a similar way, you have to brush your teeth consistently to keep them spotless and sound, you have to ponder reliably to keep your brain calm and certain.

The investigations I connected above were directed on subjects who ruminated each day for a multi-week time frame. I imagine that you'll see a perceptible distinction (regarding your capacity to avoid your head and feel increasingly certain) after around fourteen days...yet don't hope to ponder today and wake up with superhuman level confidence first thing tomorrow morning.

The best method to manufacture the day to day propensity for meditation (and see snappy outcomes) is to make it a piece of your daily schedule. I'm a huge supporter of morning schedules, and I emphatically suggest that you make a morning schedule.

Step #3: Use Mindful Breathing (When Anxious)

By following advances #1 and #2 above, and effectively fabricating the propensity for meditation, you'll build up calm confidence that will remain with you regardless of what you're doing. By this, I imply that you will normally have less self-ruinous contemplations and for the most part feel progressively certain, yet I accept that you'll forfeit a stunning advantage of meditation if you don't deliberately apply care to your life amid stress.

This is what I mean:

Envision that you're in a distressing social circumstance similar to when you notice a charming young lady you need to approach at the bar. Be that as it may, rather than making a proper acquaintance, you get apprehensive and begin to worry. You begin thinking about a lot of reasons not to move toward her, or how you could mess it all up.

Or, on the other hand, you're sitting at home and you begin to examine something that is at the forefront of your thoughts. Perhaps it's whether you ought to request an advancement at work. Maybe it's the reason that a young lady you just messaged hasn't reacted at this point.

In any case, you lose all sense of direction in a hurricane of negative contemplations, become incapacitated, and feel like a total idiot.

This is what you ought to do:

- Discover yourself becoming mixed up in negative musings.

- Concentrate on your breathing. (as you're completing a smaller than expected meditation.)

- Loosen up your body. (particularly your shoulders, neck, and chest.)

- Make a move. (do your thought process or proceed onward and accomplish something different.)

This basic practice (I like to call it 'SOS breathing') resembles a moment drug to calm pressure and take out uneasiness. You don't have to ruminate normally to utilize this apparatus, however, it's much more progressively viable (and works way speedier) in case you're thinking about an everyday schedule.

What's more, there you have it: meditation encourages you to wreck negative self-talk, which lets you quit overthinking things and be far more positive about each circumstance! The way to exploiting this reality is to figure out how to do a basic meditation that works for you, and afterward transform it into a day to day propensity.

When you're open to sitting peacefully with your reflections for five to ten minutes, it turns out to be exceptionally simple to find yourself getting on the edge and overthink about things at the same time. You can rapidly practice care, stop the negative self-talk, and turn on your regular confidence!

92

SECTION 2–ROAD TO SELF-ESTEEM

CHAPTER 8

IMPROVING SELF-ESTEEM

Self-esteem is how you feel about yourself, or the sentiment you have about yourself. Everybody has times when they feel somewhat low or think that its difficult to have faith in themselves. If this turns into a drawn-out circumstance, this can prompt issues, including emotional wellness issues like melancholy or nervousness. A portion of the side effects of low self-esteem can also be an indication of these issues.

Self-esteem is regularly a mind-blowing aftereffect of encounters, and especially what befell us when we were younger. In any case, it is conceivable to improve your self-esteem at any age. This page gives more information about self-esteem and a few steps that you can make to improve it.

Understanding Self-Esteem

A few people consider self-esteem as their inward voice (or self-discourse)—the voice that discloses to you whether you are sufficient to do or accomplish something.

Self-esteem is about how we esteem ourselves, and our pictures about what our identity is and what we can do.

Self-Esteem Isn't About Capacity
Self-esteem is regularly not related to either your capacity or others' pictures of you.

It is very workable for somebody who is acceptable at something to have poor self-esteem. On the other hand, somebody who battles with a specific undertaking may have great self-esteem.

Individuals with great self-esteem commonly feel positive about themselves and about existence. This makes them considerably more versatile, and better ready to adapt to life's high points and low points.

Those with poor self-esteem, be that as it may, are substantially more condemning of themselves. They think that it's harder to skip once again from difficulties and mishaps. This may lead them to stay away from troublesome circumstances. That can, in any case, really decline their self-esteem even more since they feel much more terrible about themselves.

An absence of self-esteem can impact how individuals carry on and also what they accomplish in their lives.

For What Reason Do People Experience Low Self-Esteem?
There are numerous reasons why somebody may have low self-esteem. It frequently begins in youth, maybe with an inclination that you couldn't satisfy hopes. It can also be the aftereffect of adult encounters, for example, a troublesome relationship either close to home or work.

Self-Esteem, Domestic Violence, and Abuse
The survivors of domestic violence and abuse frequently have low self-esteem.

This might be because their abuser has invested energy deprecating them and causing them to feel awful about themselves while decreasing their self-esteem. In any case, it might also be that their low self-esteem made them defenseless against being manhandled because they didn't feel that they were important.

No one ought to experience the ill effects of abuse or viciousness.

If you or anybody you know is in this circumstance, you should look for help.

In the UK, wellsprings of help incorporate Childline, so phone 0800 1111. The NSPCC and the National Domestic Violence Helpline is 0808 2000 247.

In the US, Government counsel is where you can call the Domestic Violence Hotline on 800-799-SAFE (7233).

Upsetting life occasions like separation or deprivation can also affect your self-esteem.

Ways to Improve Your Self-Esteem

There are various manners which you can improve your self-esteem.

1. Distinguish and Challenge Your Negative Beliefs
The initial step is to distinguish, and afterward challenge, your negative convictions about yourself.

Notice your musings about yourself. For instance, you may end up with an intuition of, 'I'm not sharp enough to do that', or 'I have no companions'. At the point when you do, search for proof that repudiates those announcements. Record both articulation and proof, and hold glancing back at it to advise yourself that your negative convictions about yourself are false.

2. Distinguish the Positive About Yourself

It is also a smart thought to record positive things about yourself like being good at a game, or decent compliments that people have said about you. At the point when you begin to feel low, glance back at these things, and advise yourself that there is a lot of good about you.

As a rule, a positive inward exchange is a major piece of improving your self-esteem. If you find yourself making statements like 'I'm sufficiently bad', or 'I'm a disappointment', you can begin to make something happen by saying, "I can beat this" and "I can turn out to be sure by reviewing myself in a positive manner."

If you find yourself falling, go into the old negative propensities, yet with customary exertion, you can begin to feel more positive and construct your self-esteem too.

3. Manufacture Positive Relationships—and Avoid Negative Ones
You will presumably find that there are sure individuals—and certain connections—that cause you to feel superior to other people.

If there are individuals who cause you to feel awful about yourself, attempt to maintain a strategic distance from them.

Assemble associations with individuals who cause you to feel great about yourself and maintain a strategic distance from the connections that drag you down.

4. Offer Yourself A Reprieve
You don't need to be ideal each hour. You don't need to like yourself constantly.

Self-esteem differs from circumstance to circumstance, from every day, and hour to hour. A few people feel loose and positive with companions and associates, yet uncomfortable and modest with outsiders. Others may feel in order of themselves at work yet battle socially. (or the other way around.)

Offer yourself a reprieve. We all have times when we feel somewhat down or think that it's harder to keep up our self-conviction.

The key isn't to be excessively hard on yourself. Be thoughtful to yourself.

Abstain from censuring yourself to other people since this can fortify your antagonistic perspectives and give others a (perhaps bogus) contrary assessment of you.

You can assist with boosting your self-esteem by giving yourself a treat at whatever point you prevail with regards to accomplishing something hard, or only for dealing with an especially awful day.

5. Become More Assertive and Learn to Say No
Individuals with low self-esteem regularly think that it's difficult to go do things for themselves or disapprove others.

This implies they may become over-troubled at home or work since they don't prefer to decline anybody anything. In any case, this can build pressure and make it significantly harder to oversee.

Building up your assertiveness can help to improve your self-esteem. Going about as though you had confidence in yourself can assist with expanding self-conviction!

6. Improve Your Physical Health
It is a lot simpler to like ourselves when we are fit and sound.

Be that as it may, people with low self-esteem frequently disregard themselves since they don't feel that they 'have the right' to be cared for.

Take a stab at taking more exercise, eating well, and getting enough rest. It is also a smart thought to make time to unwind and to accomplish something that you need to do, as opposed to something that another person anticipates that you should do. You may locate that basic changes like this can have an enormous effect on your general standpoint.

7. Take on Challenges
Individuals with low self-esteem frequently abstain from testing and troublesome circumstances.

One approach to improve your self-esteem can be to take on a test. This doesn't imply that you have to do everything yourself—some portion of the test may be to look for help when you need it—yet be set up to have a go at something that you realize will be hard to accomplish.

By succeeding, you give yourself what you can accomplish.

These difficulties on your negative convictions will improve your self-esteem.

Self-Awareness

Self-mindfulness is one of the key segments of emotional knowledge (EI).

Daniel Goleman, the master of emotional insight, distinguished self-awareness as being comprised of emotional awareness, precise self-evaluation, and self-confidence. At the end of the day, it is tied in with knowing your emotions, your qualities and shortcomings, and having your very own solid feeling of worth.

Individuals who need self-awareness discover living an upbeat and beneficial life. This can be hard to survive. The same number of social orders and societies urge us to disregard our sentiments and emotions, which makes us 'resist the urge to panic'.

Examples of this include people who remain in occupations that they discover unfulfilling or make them miserable, or seeing someone who is not happy.

Emotional Awareness
Emotional awareness is the capacity to perceive your own emotions and their belongings. Individuals who have this capacity will:

- Comprehend what emotions they feel at some random time, and why;

- Comprehend the connections between their emotions and their musings and activities, including what they state;

- See how their emotions will consequently influence their presentation; and

- Be guided by the way they feel by their qualities.

Being mindful of your own emotions and how they influence your conduct. It is critical to consider cooperation with others. Be that as it may, it can also be urgent to your well-being.

Living Without Emotional Awareness

A few people discover approaches to cover their emotions as opposed to tuning in to them.

Dependence on specific practices is frequently connected to emotional veiling. These incorporate inordinate drinking and over-eating, over-working, PC games, betting, practice, and whatever other exercises that viably divert the psyche.

Individuals can find self-investigation of their emotions troublesome, particularly if they have smothered them for a while. It might be difficult for individuals to perceive their emotions and also find it significantly hard to comprehend why they are feeling them.

Self-examination is an indispensable expertise to learn and produces good emotional insight.

A decent beginning stage is to know about your qualities, which can also be thought of as your own 'ethical compass'.

These qualities have an emotional incentive to us, which in this way implies numerous emotional reactions that originate from some activity or occasion of those qualities.

If you know about your qualities, you can rapidly observe why you may have had an especially emotional response to an occasion or individual.

In particular, you would then be able to make a move to address the issue with a superior comprehension of the issue.

Precise Self-Assessment

Understanding your own and other people's emotions also require a decent comprehension of your qualities, shortcomings, inward assets, and your cutoff points.

It tends to be especially difficult to admit to shortcomings and cutoff points, particularly if you are in a serious and quick-moving workplace, however, it is urgent for emotional insight and your well-being.

Individuals who are acceptable at self-evaluation will not only have a decent comprehension of their qualities and shortcomings, they will also show a decent comical inclination about themselves and their restrictions. They are normally intelligent and open to feedback.

Caution! Vulnerable Sides

It very well may be difficult to admit to shortcomings, and numerous individuals could likely be in a condition of refusal that they have any, particularly for those in senior positions. It can also be difficult to get authentic, productive feedback. These outcomes in 'vulnerable sides', issue regions that are imperceptible to the individual concerned.

Regular 'vulnerable sides' recognized in an investigation of senior officials include:

Defining unreasonable objectives for oneself or the association, and having ridiculous thoughts of how effectively assignments could be practiced; 'Dazzle desire', where the individual must be 'right' consistently; and difficult work, working extended periods, and being in danger of burnout, can cause these vulnerable sides can make an individual extremely impervious to feedback. This makes it considerably harder to beat the issue.

The arrangement? Start looking for standard and legit feedback from everyone around you—and afterward follow up on it.

Self-Confidence
The last zone of self-mindfulness is self-confidence, having your very own solid feeling self-worth, and not depending on others for your valuation of yourself.

Individuals with great self-confidence are:

- Ready to introduce themselves well, and are frequently depicted as alluring.

- Arranged to voice disagreeable assessments, and don't generally 'take the path of least resistance'.

- Confident and are ready to use sound judgment based on their qualities.

- Self-confidence is completely indispensable for work execution.

Without the capacity to 'come out with the simple truth when it is important, and to go out for disliked positions, it is difficult to accomplish anything, particularly during extreme occasions.

Self-Motivation

Self-motivation is, in its easiest structure, the power that drives you to get things done.

The subject of self-motivation, in any case, is a long way from being straightforward. Individuals can be propelled by numerous things, both interior and outside, like wanting to accomplish something, love of somebody, or requirement for cash. As a rule, motivation is a consequence of a few elements.

The capacity to propel yourself—self-motivation—is a significant ability. Self-motivation drives individuals to prop up even with setbacks, to accept up open doors, and to demonstrate the promise of what they need to accomplish.

What is Motivation?

Motivation is the thing that pushes us to accomplish our objectives, feel progressively satisfied, and improve our general personal satisfaction.

Motivation is one of the three zones of individual abilities that are indispensable to the idea of emotional insight.

Daniel Goleman, the writer of a few fundamental books on Emotional Intelligence, distinguished four components that make up motivation:

- Individual drive to accomplish the craving to improve or satisfy certain guidelines;

- Pledge to individual or hierarchical objectives;

- Activity, which he characterized as 'status to follow up on circumstances'; and

- Good faith, the capacity to continue onward, and seek after objectives without difficulties. This is also called versatility.

To develop self-motivation, it is supportive to see more about these individual components.

The Elements of Self-Motivation

1. Individual Drive To Accomplish

You could think about an individual drive to accomplish as desire, or could be closer to home strengthening. Nonetheless, it is also worth considering it regarding attitude.

There are two sorts of mentality, fixed and development.

Those with a fixed outlook accept that ability is instilled, and that we can't change our degree of capacity.

Those with a development outlook accept that they can improve their aptitudes through difficult work and exertion.

Research shows that individuals who accept what they can improve in—that is, who have a development attitude—are unmistakably bound to accomplish anything in whatever circle they pick. A development mentality is subsequently a significant component in an individual's drive to succeed.

Different components of individual drive incorporate being sorted out, especially being acceptable at that time and staying away from interruptions.

2. Responsibility to Objectives

There is impressive proof—regardless of whether or not if it is episodic—that the objective setting is critical to our general well-being.

If you need to carry on with an upbeat life, attach it to an objective, not to individuals or things.

"You cannot achieve a new goal by applying the same level of thinking that got you where you are today."
- Albert Einstein

"The greatest danger for most of us is not that our aim is too high and we miss it, but that it is too low and we reach it."
- Michelangelo

"If you aim at nothing, you will hit it every time." If you don't set goals for your life then it's almost certain that you will be very disappointed with your results. Aiming at nothing is setting yourself up to achieve nothing.
–Zig Ziglar

3. Activity

Activity is the capacity to make the most of chances when they happen.

It is very simple to waver, and afterward, the open door might be gone. Be that as it may, the familiar adages 'look before you jump' and 'dolts surge in where blessed messengers dread to step' have a ton of truth in them. It is also essential to thoroughly consider things and guarantee that you are settling on the correct choice for you.

Activity can be considered as a blend of fearlessness. Hazard the executives is important to guarantee that you recognize the correct chances to consider and that they have the fitting degree of hazard for you, and boldness is important to conquer the dread of the obscure characteristics in new chances.

4. Idealism or Versatility

Idealism is the capacity to look on the brilliant side or think positively. Strength is the capacity to 'bob back' after a mishap, or keep positive challenges. The two are firmly related, even though it is not the equivalent. Versatile individuals utilize their capacity to think as an approach to oversee negative emotional reactions to occasions. At the end of the day, they utilize positive or normal intuition to look at, and if fundamental, conquer responses that they comprehend may not be altogether coherent. They are also arranged to request help if it's important—just to offer their assistance when others are out of luck.

Kinds of Motivators: Intrinsic and Extrinsic Motivators
In pondering self-motivation, it is useful to comprehend what rouses you to get things done.

There are two primary sorts of inspirations: 'intrinsic' and 'extrinsic'.

In their most straightforward structure, you can consider these two sorts of motivations as:

- Intrinsic = identified with what we need to do from the inside of the individual.

- Extrinsic = identified with what we need to do from the outside world.

A progressive point by point definition is:

Intrinsic motivation: involves engaging in a behavior because it is personally rewarding; essentially, performing an activity for its own sake rather than the desire for some external reward. Essentially, the behavior itself is its own reward.

Extrinsic motivation: occurs when we are motivated to perform a behavior or engage in an activity to earn a reward or avoid punishment. In this case, you engage in behavior not because you enjoy it or because you find it satisfying, but in order to get something in return or avoid something unpleasant.

Various people are inspired by various things on various occasions in their lives. A similar assignment may have created natural sparks on specific occasions and made outward inspirations to others, and most errands have a blend of the two sorts of motivation.

Model:

John works since he needs to pay his home loan and feed himself and his family. He gets no fulfillment from his activity and there is no way of advancement. John's inspirations are simply outward.

Sally works since she adores what she does. She gets tremendous fulfillment and self-satisfaction from her work. Sally has enough cash set aside that she doesn't have to work, so she possesses her own home and can bear to purchase what she needs when she needs it. Sally's helpers are just not needed.

Obviously, Sally and John are in various parts of the bargain motivation range. The vast majority, in any case, falls somewhere in the center.

Many people accomplish the need to work and to win cash, yet they also discover their everyday work life or fulfilling in other natural manners like work fulfillment and the opportunity to associate with partners.

As a whole, we tend to work better when we love what we are doing.

It's simpler to get up toward the beginning of the day, we are more joyful in our work, and more joyful when all is said and done.

Research shows this is especially significant when we're under pressure. It's a lot simpler to adapt to pressure and extended lengths of time if we, for the most part, appreciate the work. Natural sparks in this manner have a major influence on self-motivation for the greater part of us.

The Importance of Obligation
What if an objective has neither intrinsic or extrinsic motivators?

The undeniable end is that we are probably not going to do it since it will be futile. We realize it doesn't generally work that way. There is a further issue: sentiments of obligation.

Obligation inspirations are not either inborn or outward, however, it can be ground-breaking. Obligation originates from our morals and feeling of obligation, what is correct, and what's up.

An obligation simply insists that you have to carry out a task or responsibility, even when you don't want to or feel like doing so.

You may feel obliged to go to a gathering since you were welcomed by someone you know, but there will be no conspicuous outward or natural advantage to you joining in, however, you may stress that you will affront or upset your companion if you don't go. You are bound to appreciate the gathering if you go with a positive and open demeanor, anticipating that it should be enjoyable. This includes a characteristic spark: fun and delight.

The Skills You Need to Guide Yourself to Personal Development
Figure out how to set yourself viable individual objectives and discover the motivation you have to accomplish them. This is the substance of self-improvement. A lot of abilities intended to assist you with arriving at your maximum capacity, at work, in your study, and in your own life.

Slowly and carefully turning out to be self-roused, or even simply improving your self-motivation a bit, won't occur incidentally.

There are numerous aptitudes included, and you can't hope to create them all in a split second. A superior comprehension of the components of motivation, and especially how they all fit together, should assist with expanding your aptitudes. Remember, Rome was not built in a day: consider gaining ground over a significant period and in little advance.

CHAPTER 9
DEALING WITH CRITICISM

Managing criticism positively is a significant fundamental ability. Sooner or later in your life, you will be criticized, maybe in a professional way. Now and then it will be hard to acknowledge, however, that all relies upon your response.

You can either positively utilize criticism to improve, or in a negative way it can bring down your self-esteem and cause pressure, outrage, or even hostility.

To manage criticism positively you may require great self-esteem and some assertiveness aptitudes.

There are two kinds of criticism, which are both —valuable and damaging. Figuring out how to perceive the contrast between the two can assist you in managing any criticism you may get.

Anybody can reprimand, denounce, and grumble, yet it takes character and self-control to be understanding.

When tested by someone else, it is entirely expected to respond negatively. Consider how negative responses make you look and how they affect you. The way you decide to deal with criticism has a ton of impact in different parts of your life. Subsequently, it is smarter to distinguish manners by which you can profit by criticism and use it to further your potential benefit to be a more grounded and progressively capable individual.

Constructive and Destructive Criticism

The contrast between valuable criticism and damaging criticism is how remarks are conveyed.

Even though the two structures are testing your thoughts, character, or capacity, when somebody is giving ruinous criticism it can hurt your pride and effectively affect your self-esteem and confidence. Damaging criticism is regularly only negligence by someone else, however, it can also be intentionally malevolent and pernicious. Destructive criticism can, every now and again, lead to outrage or potentially, animosity.

Constructive criticism is intended to call attention to your slip-ups, yet it also shows you where and how upgrades can be made. Constructive criticism ought to be seen as valuable feedback that can assist you with developing yourself instead of putting you down.

At the point when criticism is valuable, it is typically simpler to acknowledge, regardless of whether everything is harmful. In either situation, consistently attempt to recollect so that you can utilize criticism to further your potential benefit.

> "He who covers his sins will not prosper, but whoever confesses and forsakes them will have mercy.".
>
> - Proverbs 28:13

Managing Critical People

Some people are just critical by nature and don't generally understand that they are offending the feelings of someone else.

If you know an individual who is critical of everything, do whatever it takes not to pay attention to their remarks as well, as this is simply part of their character quality. If you do acknowledge adverse remarks it could instigate hatred and outrage towards the other individual, which could harm the relationship.

Keep in mind, individuals who scrutinize everything or offer searing comments to be terrible are the ones that need assistance—not you!

How you truly respond to criticism will rely upon the idea of the criticism, where you are, and who the criticism is originating from.

The key thing to recollect is that whatever the situation is, don't react out of resentment as this will create an uproar and make awful sentiments—and conceivably paint an awful picture of you.

Attempt to stay cool and approach the other individual with deference and comprehension. This will assist with defusing the circumstance and possibly prevent it from turning crazy. Show that you are the more grounded individual and make an effort not to fall for the trap, don't utilize it as motivation to offer counter-criticism. If you challenge the other individual you may begin a contention that is most likely superfluous.

If you do feel that you may lose self-control, or state or accomplish something conceivably harming, leave. If you are in a gathering at work, considerately pardon yourself and leave the room until you have had the opportunity to assemble yourself. Even though someone's negative comments may hurt, it is unsafe for you to permit their criticism to be ruinous to your confidence.

Taking the Positives From Criticism

We as a whole commit error constantly, it is human instinct. As we experience life we have a lot of chances to learn and develop ourselves. Along these lines, regardless of what sort of criticism is focused on you, break it down to discover something you can gain from. In material issues at work, school, or social clubs attempt to accept criticism to enable you to improve. At the point when someone is assaulting your character it is difficult to acknowledge, however, that doesn't mean you ought to disregard it.

Also remember that the criticism focused on you may not bode well at that point. For the most part talking, there is a trace of validity in criticism to be given in a spirit of meanness and sharpness. It is frequent that the situation has a slight affect on your character and is a reasonable impression of how someone else sees you by then. Make a stride back and attempt to see things from the other individual's perspective, maybe approach a companion for their legit supposition. Use criticism admirably and as a learning experience. Check whether it is conceivable to find out a little about how others see you. You might have the option to utilize criticism to improve your relational abilities.

We all learn by committing errors, and figuring out how to manage criticism positively is one way that we can improve our relational associations with others.

Offering Constructive Criticism
Criticism is characterized by Chambers English Dictionary as 'condemning' someone else.

Its unique sense may well have been both positive and negative, in a similar sense that a theater pundit can give a positive audit.

There is no doubt, in any case, that the greater part of us would see individual criticism as negative.

'Criticism' may be viewed as another word for 'negative feedback'. The feedback section discloses how to make your basic investigation of others 'constructive', with the goal that you set up for enhancements as opposed to 'damaging', which could 'wreck' the other individual.

Destructive and Constructive Criticism
Destructive criticism offers no assistance or backing for development. It just sets out the issue observed by the individual giving criticism. It is typically communicated as a remark about the beneficiary, their aptitudes or characteristics, and not their conduct. You can consider it having a tendency to cut somebody down, and causing them to feel terrible, regardless of whether this is purposeful or not.

Constructive criticism, then again, recognizes manners by which the beneficiary can make changes that improve matters. It develops the other individual and encourages them to roll out positive improvements to their conduct in order to stay away from future issues.

The most ideal approach to offer constructive criticism is to consider it as 'negative feedback', and consistently adhere to the standards about giving feedback.

Rules for Giving Feedback

1. Constructive Criticism Focuses on Behavior.
Great feedback, regardless of whether positive or negative, centers around conduct.

It ought not to be about what the other individual is, or what they accept, yet what they did. Constructive criticism makes this one stride further and centers around the conduct that you need, not the conduct that you saw and didn't appreciate.

Top Tip For Constructive Feedback:

- Rather than saying something like: "Kindly don't do that, I truly detest it",

- Have a go at saying: "I would truly like it if you would do this, rather than that, as it would have an x impact".

Feedback or criticism framed in these terms is a lot simpler to acknowledge and follows up on what it says unmistakably and if that conduct would be better, and offers an answer or alternatives for change.

2. Great Feedback Focuses on the Effect on You, Not on the Other Person's Intentions
This isn't selfishness, yet a basic understanding that you don't have the foggiest idea about what the other individual proposed or thought, is just the impact that it had on you.

It is consequently accommodating if you can give your feedback regarding the impact that it had on you. For instance, you may state, "When you do that, I feel like this".

Constructive criticism takes this further and centers around the conduct that is important to prompt better sentiments.

Top Tip For Constructive Feedback:

- Try not to state: "At the point when you do that, it causes me to feel this way",

- Rather, have a go at saying: "If you somehow managed to do x, I figure it would cause me to be feely".

3. Powerful Feedback Needs to be Very Specific
Great feedback is as explicit as could reasonably be expected. The more definite you can be about the conduct that you need to see, the simpler it is for the other individual to do it.

You don't have to state what conduct you don't care for: rather, you can have a go at inquiring as to whether the other individual would be set up to accomplish something other than what's expected.

Have a go at requesting that the other individual do what you might want as a straightforward kindness. It doesn't need to be a remark on their past conduct by any stretch of the imagination.

Use phrases like: "Okay, mind doing x?", or "It would be ideal if you will you do y? It would be so useful".

These may not offer long haul arrangements, however, it will appear, rapidly and successfully with what you might want them to do.

You can also trust that they will accept it as an enduring change.

4. Feedback Needs to be Given Promptly
It's horrible hauling up old occasions long after they had passed.

To be compelling, feedback and criticism should be pretty quick, while the occasions are still new in everybody's brains.

All things considered, in case you're irate about what's occurred, it's best to hold up until you are more settled since this will empower you to keep the discussion constructive.

Top Tip For **Constructive** Criticism

- Try not to get frantic, settle the score!

- No, you're not hoping to get your retribution, yet quieten down and recover your relationship in any event.

- Try not to be enticed to condemn when you're irate. It won't be lovely, and it won't be constructive.

5. Feedback Must Be Heard to Be Effective
This keeps from the last principle: you have to give feedback, especially negative feedback when the other individual is prepared to hear it.

It's awful doing it when both of you are irate, or when you're worn out, or not prepared to hear undesirable news.

Walk a Mile in the Other Person's Shoes
Most importantly, before you give any sort of criticism or negative feedback, consider how you might want to hear similar kinds of information.

Would what you need to say to be worthy for you?

Ask yourself truly and consider the appropriate response.

If you are extremely certain that you would think that it's satisfactory, you should give that bit of criticism in that manner. Something else, it's presumably best to return to the standards on this page and discover another way.

Giving and Receiving Feedback

In life as much as in work, it's critical to realize how to give feedback to other people, successfully and constructively without causing offenses.

There are numerous open doors in life for furnishing others with feedback, from remarking in transit that your associate has done an errand to examining your child's conduct with them.

This section centers around the way toward speaking with somebody about something that they have done or stated, with the end goal of changing or empowering that conduct. This is frequently called 'giving feedback', and when you do, you need your feedback to be successful.

'Feedback' is a utilized term for the correspondence hypothesis.

What is Effective Feedback?

For our motivations, we will characterize powerful feedback which is unmistakably heard, comprehended, and acknowledged. Those are territories that are within your capacity. You do not influence whether the beneficiary decides to follow up on your feedback, so how about we put that to the other side?

So how might you ensure that your feedback is successful?

Build up your feedback abilities by utilizing these couple of rules, and you'll find that you're considerably more compelling.

1. Feedback ought to be about conduct, not character
The first and the most significant principle of feedback is to recall that you are offering no remark on what kind of individual they are, or what they accept or esteem. You are just remarking on how they

acted. Try not to be enticed to talk about parts of character, insight, or whatever else. Just conduct.

2. Feedback ought to portray the impact of the individual's conduct on you

All things considered, you don't have a clue about the impact on anybody or whatever else. Your ability caused you to feel or what you thought. Introducing feedback as your feeling makes it a lot simpler for the beneficiary to hear and acknowledge it, regardless of whether you are giving negative feedback. They do not influence how you felt, anything else than you have any power over their expectation. This methodology is a fault-free one, which is along these lines more worthy.

Pick your feedback language cautiously.

Helpful expressions for giving feedback include:

- "At the point when you did [x], I felt [y]."

- "I saw that when you said [x], it caused me to feel [y]."

- "I truly preferred the way that you did [x] and especially [y] about it."

- "It caused me to feel truly [x] to hear you state [y] in that manner."

3. Feedback ought to be as explicit as could reasonably be expected

Particularly when things are not working out in a good way, we realize that it's enticing to begin from the perspective of 'all that you do is waste', yet don't. Consider explicit events and explicit conduct to point out precisely what the individual did, and precisely how it affected you. The more explicit, the better since it is a lot simpler to catch wind of a particular event than pretty much 'constantly'!

4. Feedback ought to be opportune
It's awfully enlightening with somebody regarding something that outraged or satisfied you half a year later. Feedback should be convenient, which implies that while everybody can recollect what occurred. If you have feedback to give, at that point you simply jump on and give it. That doesn't mean without thought though. You need to consider what you're going to state and how.

5. Pick your second
There are times when individuals are feeling open to feedback and times when they aren't. This will assist you in picking a reasonable second. For instance, an irate individual won't have any desire to acknowledge feedback, even if given skillfully. Hold up until they've quietened down a bit.

Feedback doesn't simply occur in formal feedback gatherings.

Each association is an open door for feedback in two bearings. Probably the most significant feedback may happen coolly in a fast exchange, for instance, this one caught while two associates were making espresso:

Mary (snickering): "You help me to remember my mom."

Jane (her chief): "Truly, why?"

Mary: "She gets extremely smart with me when she's focused as well."

Jane: "Goodness, I'm so heartbroken. Have I been lashing out at you? I am somewhat focused, however, I'll do whatever it takes not to do it in the future. I'm much obliged to you for letting me know, and I'm sorry you expected to."

Mary had calmly raised a genuine social issue with Jane. Jane understood that she was lucky that Mary had perceived the standard of conduct from a familial circumstance and reached her determinations.

Jane also perceived that not every person she could ever work with would do otherwise. Having been made mindful of her conduct, she decided to transform it. Mary had also, calmly or not, given feedback per the guidelines: it was about Jane's ongoing conduct, as was explicit and convenient, and demonstrated how Mary saw it. It was also at a decent second when Jane was loose and open to conversation.

Accepting Feedback
It's also essential to consider what abilities you have to get feedback, particularly when it is something you would prefer not to hear, and not least because not every person is talented at giving feedback.

Be open to feedback. To hear feedback, you have to hear it out. Try not to consider what you're going to state in answer, simply tune in. What's more, notice the non-verbal correspondence too, and tune in to what your associate isn't stating, just as what they are.

For instance, you may state: "So, when you said..., would it be reasonable to state that you implied...and felt...?", or "Have I seen accurately that when I did..., you felt...?"

Ensure that your appearance and questions center around conduct, not character. Regardless of whether the feedback has been given at another level, you can generally restore the discussion to a social conversation, and help the individual by offering feedback to concentrate on that level. Emotional insight is fundamental. You should know about your emotions (self-mindfulness) and have the option to oversee them (self-control) so that regardless of whether the feedback causes an emotional reaction, you can control it.

Also, continuously thank the individual who has given you the feedback. They have just observed that you have tuned in and acknowledged it.

Acknowledgment along these lines doesn't imply that you have to follow up on it. Be that as it may, you do need to think about the feedback, and choose how you wish to follow up on it. That is completely up to you. However, recollect that the individual giving the feedback felt emphatical enough to try referencing it to you.

Do them the kindness by giving the issue some thought. In the case of nothing else, with negative feedback, you need to know how not to produce that reaction once more.

Remember to click here to access your free gift or scan the QR code below.

And if you want a better experience you can enjoy the audiobook for free here or you can scan the QR code below

CHAPTER 10
RECOGNIZING AND MANAGING EMOTIONS

This page encourages you to perceive and comprehend your own emotions and clarifies why they are here. It offers some viable thoughts regarding how you can deal with your own emotions so you can utilize and outfit them, however, they are not totally represented by them.

What are Emotions?

Emotions are sentiments. To begin to comprehend your emotions, you have to pose yourself two inquiries:

How would I feel?

How would I know?

Other people have emotions too. Simultaneously being mindful of your own emotions, you should know about those of others.

You also need to inquire:

How would others feel, and how would I know?

There are a few different ways that we can tell how others are feeling, however, by seeing what they state and how they carry on, which includes their non-verbal communication. Research proposes that over 80% of correspondence is non-verbal, implying that it originates from non-verbal communication and outward appearance. A considerable lot of us don't prefer to discuss our emotions, particularly if they truly matter to us, so they will be communicated significantly more in our non-verbal communication.

Emotions and the Brain
Emotions are not deliberately controlled. The piece of the cerebrum that manages emotions is the limbic system. It's the idea that this piece of the mind developed genuinely from the get-go in mankind's history, making it very crude. This clarifies why an emotional reaction is frequently very clear, yet exceptionally amazing: you need to cry, or flee, or yell.

This is because these reactions are based around the need to endure.

Emotions are firmly connected to memory and experience. If something awful has recently transpired, your emotional reaction to a similar improvement is going to be solid.

Children feel emotion, yet can't to some extent. Emotions are also firmly connected to values: an emotional reaction could reveal to you that one of your key qualities has been tested.

Understanding this connection to memory and qualities gives you the way to dealing with your emotional reaction, which doesn't have a lot to do with the present circumstance, or to reason. However, you can defeat them with reason and by being mindful of your responses.

Attempt This:

Set aside some effort to see your emotional reactions and consider what may be behind them, regardless of whether esteems, recollections, or encounters.

- Also consider what brings about positive emotions and what is negative.

- Keep in mind, you can change how you feel.

Figuring Out How to Manage Emotions

Much has been said and discussed about the most proficient method to oversee and control emotions.

You can pick how you feel. - Anon

You can't control others, however, you can control how you respond to them. - Anon.

"Anybody can become angry - that is easy, but to be angry with the right person and to the right degree and at the right time and for the right purpose, and in the right way - that is not within every-body's power and is not easy."

- Aristotle

The lattice beneath shows the harmony among high and low, and negative and positive power:

- High positive power empowers you to perform well, yet you can't remain in that state forever. Eventually, you have to lessen the power. Remain positive, and you will recuperate rapidly. Plunge into negative emotions and you will get a handle of being consumed.

- High negative power is a significant awkward spot to be: it feels like you're constantly battling for endurance. Once more, you should diminish the power sooner or later since it could prompt burnout.

Positive Actions to Help You Manage Emotions
There are various moves that you can make that will assist you in managing your emotions. A significant number of them are exceptionally broad, yet attempt them since you may simply find that they work.

- Exercise: this discharges prize and joy synthetics in the mind, for example, dopamine, which causes you to feel better. Being fit also makes you more beneficial, which helps in overseeing emotions.

- Be caring for other people since this helps stop you from agonizing over yourself.

- Be open and acknowledge what is happening around you. Figure out how to acknowledge what's going on and stay away from over the top criticism of others or circumstances. This is connected to care, which is tied in with being mindful of what is happening at the time.

- It's acceptable to talk. Invest energy with others and appreciate their conversation.

- Occupy yourself. Indeed, you truly are that shallow. Watching a bit of TV, perusing, or riding the web will presumably assist you with forgetting that you were feeling somewhat down.

- Try not to surrender to negative reasoning. If you end up having negative considerations, at that point challenge them by searching for proof against them.

- Invest energy outside. Being in the outside air, particularly around nature, is exceptionally useful for quieting the emotions. There is proof that we have to see skylines, so if you can go up a slope and take a look at the view, that point do.

- Be thankful. Thank individuals face to face for doing pleasant things for you and recollect it.

- Play to your qualities. That frequently implies doing things that you appreciate, however, it also includes doing things that are beneficial for you.

- Notice the beneficial things throughout your life. In antiquated terms, remember your good fortune.

This rundown may sound very good, yet maybe our grandparents knew things about overseeing emotions that we may have overlooked. Finding the correct parity for you can help decrease your feelings of anxiety may help battle sadness.

Applying Reason to Emotion
As we said above, you can change how you feel. The key is to know about your emotional reaction, and comprehend what may be behind it. That way, you can apply some motivation to the circumstance.

For instance, you may pose yourself a few inquiries about potential game-plans as:

- What is my opinion about this circumstance?

- What do I figure I ought to do about it?

- What impact would that have for me and others?

Assume you're afraid of being left in the dark because you once got locked inside a dark room when you were a child.

You also have an emotional reaction to the dark due to your previous experience. In any case, you can advise yourself that you are currently an adult and that there is nothing to scare you. You should simply stroll over to the light and turn it on.

By rehearsing this, you can assist your cerebrum with the understanding that there is nothing to be terrified about and gradually retrain your limbic system.

Making Decisions With Emotions
At the point when you decide, you can draw on reason, emotion, or a blend of the two.

Emotional decisions are observed as made 'without giving it much thought', however, emotions have a more prominent influence in many decisions than we might know. In case you're hitched, for instance, you'll realize that an impressive idea may go into the decision about whether to get hitched. Not many would contend that the decision is made exclusively based on rationale.

The best decisions are made utilizing both rationale and emotion.

If you just utilize either, your decisions may either not be adjusted, or not bolster your emotional needs. Rather, you have to join your emotional reaction with sound contemplations.

You can do this by:

- Halting before you choose, to allow yourself to think.

- Consider how you will feel because of every conceivable activity.

- Consider what may occur and how your decision may influence others. Be content with those impacts.

- Take a break before settling on a decision.

- Think about the decision against your qualities. Does it fit with them? If not, why not?

Consider what somebody whom you regard with would think about your decision. Is it true that you are content with that?

At long last, consider what might occur if everybody somehow happened to make a similar move. If this would be a debacle, and at that point, it is best not to do it.

Emotions are Important
It pays to know about our own and other people's sentiments. Emotionally, insightful individuals do this all the time. Like some other, it is an ability that can be created and is well worth gaining.

I've discovered that individuals will overlook what you stated, individuals will overlook what you did, however, individuals will always remember how you affected them.

Maya Angelou

Anger Management 101

Anger is a superbly ordinary human emotion and when managed properly, sound. Be that as it may, you should have the option to deal with your anger. It is neither fitting nor solid if you can't remain calm and frequently lash out at others.

Uncontrolled and visit upheavals of anger will influence your well-being and your associations with others.

Anger management is a term used to depict the abilities you have to perceive that you, or another person, is losing control. Afterward, make suitable moves to manage the circumstance in a positive manner. It doesn't mean disguising or smothering anger, however, perceiving the triggers and indications of anger, and finding other suitable approaches to communicate our sentiments is essential.

Control However Don't Suppress
Anger management is tied in with figuring out how to control your anger.

This doesn't intend to smother or disguise it, which can be as harming as incessant upheavals. Rather, it is tied in with understanding why you are furious, and figuring out how to deal with your emotions. It is, in this manner, a significant component of self-control.

We blow-up every now and again, even individuals who are generally well-tempered. It is acceptable to be irate here and there: for instance, at shamefulness, or when somebody's privileges are encroached on. It is an essential piece of life.

The man who presents the correct things and with the ideal individuals, and, further, as he should when he should, and as long as he should, is lauded.

Aristotle

The way to anger is to figure out how to oversee it with the goal that it may be diverted into suitable activity. Anger management abilities will assist you with understanding what is behind your anger, and afterward, express it in a progressively solid manner. This will permit you to convey your message more plainly.

A considerable lot of us have learned practices to assist us with managing forceful emotions. Anger management may be tied in with unlearning insufficient ways of dealing with stress and re-learning positive approaches to manage the issues and dissatisfactions that lead to anger.

Do You Need Professional Help With Your Anger?
There are many anger management strategies that you can learn and rehearse without anyone else or instruct other people. If you, or somebody you know encounter a great deal of standard or solid anger (rage) at that point you might need to look for help from a guide.

You should look for proficient assistance if anger is having a drawn-out negative effect on your connections, is making you troubled, or is bringing about any dangerous or savage conduct.

If any of these announcements are valid for you, at that point you may require proficient assistance to deal with your anger.

- Your conduct has prompted any kind of criminal or common bad behavior.

- You are brutal towards your accomplice, children, or others.

- You undermine viciousness to individuals or property.

- You have upheavals of fury which include intentionally breaking things.

- You have consistent contentions with individuals near you, your life partner/accomplice, guardians, children, associates, or companions.

- You feel furious now and again, but disguise your emotion.

- You believe that you may require proficient assistance with your anger.

Steps Towards Anger Management

There are various advances that we can all take to assist us in managing our anger better.

Stage 1: Begin to Understand Your Anger
Anger is an emotion like some other, and the initial move towards being ready to control any emotion is to comprehend why it occurs.

Numerous individuals use anger as an approach to conceal different emotions, for example, dread, weakness, or humiliation. This is especially valid for individuals who were not urged to communicate their emotions as a child, however, it can apply to anybody.

At the point when you begin to feel furious, look behind your anger to check whether you can recognize what you are truly feeling.

When you name the inclination, you will think that it's simpler to communicate it properly.

Stage 2: Know Your Triggers and Signs
We have certain things that drive us mad and indications that we are beginning to lose our temper.

Figuring out how to perceive both can make it simpler to stop before you lose control.

The indications of anger are regularly simpler to perceive. For instance, individuals regularly state that their pulse increments when they are irate, because anger is connected to the adrenaline (fight or flight) reaction. You may also find that your breathing speeds up for a similar explanation. You may tense your muscles—individuals regularly hold their clench hands when they are irate. A few people need to move around, pacing the floor—once more as an adrenaline reaction.

Triggers are frequently close to home, however, various general subjects can assist you with identifying them. For instance:

Negative idea designs are frequently connected with irate upheavals. Be careful if you begin once again summing him up ("Never causes me!", "She generally leaves her shoes lying about!"), or making a hasty judgment about what individuals are thinking.

Individuals or spots that you discover upsetting may also make it harder to control your emotions. If your anger is a cover for different emotions, it might develop. Being mindful of what makes you pushed can assist you with avoiding those circumstances, or request help to oversee them better.

Stage 3: Learn Ways to Cool Down Your Temper
Similarly, we have triggers for anger, so we have ways that we can 'chill off'. Learning a few methods implies you can utilize them when you notice your obvious anger signs.

Some valuable methods include intentionally breathing slowly and relax. The thought behind this is to attempt to switch a portion of the physical side effects of anger.

<u>A Breathing Exercise</u>
At the point when you begin to feel tense and irate, attempt to seclude yourself for fifteen minutes and focus on unwinding and quiet, consistent relaxation:

- Breathe in and breathe out multiple times in succession.

- Count gradually to four and breathe in.

- Count gradually to eight you breathe out.

- Concentrate on feeling the air move all through your lungs.

- Concentrate and feel your ribs gradually rise and fall as you rehash the activity.

- Stop and return to typical breathing if you begin to feel bleary-eyed.

Regardless of whether you can't remove yourself for fifteen minutes, halting and taking (and especially discharging) some full breaths can assist you with relaxing and allow you to think.

<u>Concentrate on How You Feel Physically</u>
Pause for a minute to see your body's responses. What has befallen your relaxing? Your pulse? What else has changed?

Some of the time, simply seeing the physical changes in your body can assist with quietening you down, because it turns your psyche to some different option from the quick issue.

Gradually Count to Ten (or More!)

Allow rationale to find your emotions.

Counting to ten (ideally in your mind, particularly if you are with others) before saying or doing anything will assist you with avoiding saying anything you may later lament. It will also assist you in working out how best to convey the desired information.

Stretch: if you are angry, you tend to tense up. Gradually stretching out can help you ease off the pressure a little bit, which again overturns some of the physical signs of anger and makes you feel more relaxed.

Step 4: Find Other Ways to Express Your Anger
There are times when anger is fitting, but detonating isn't. You have to locate a sound method to communicate your anger in tranquility, and with the goal that your message is heard.

A few different ways to guarantee that this happens include:

- Plan 'Troublesome' Conversations.

If you are stressed over having a discussion that may leave you feeling furious at some point, attempt to assume responsibility for the circumstance. Make notes in advance, arranging what you need to state quietly and emphatically. You are more averse to get diverted in your discussion if you can allude to your notes.

- Concentrate on Solutions not Problems.

Instead of dwelling on what has driven you crazy, give centering a shot on how to determine issues so they don't emerge again later on.

- Give Yourself Time.

Hold up until you have quietened down from your anger and afterward communicate in a quiet and gathered manner. You should be self-assured without being aggressive.

<u>Concentrate on the Relationship, and Don't Hold Grudges</u>
We need to acknowledge that everyone is unique and how we can't control the emotions, convictions, or practices of others.

Rather than concentrating on the prompt issue, center around the relationship. This is a higher priority than who is 'correct'. Attempt to be sensible and acknowledge that individuals are how they are, not how we might want them to be. Being angry or holding resentment against someone will expand your anger and make it harder to control. You can't change how others carry on or think, however, you can change how you manage others and take a shot at a positive mentality.

- Use Humor to Defuse Situations.

It is anything but difficult to utilize improper mockery when furious; oppose the compulsion to do this and deal with bringing some geniality into troublesome discussions. If you can present some humor, hatred will be diminished and your temperament lifted.

The basic demonstration of snickering can go far to diminish anger, particularly over the more drawn out term.

Stage 5: Care for Yourself
Any sort of emotional management is simpler if you are well and solid as a main priority and body.

Or, on the other hand, when we are under pressure—which incorporates being unfortunate—it is more diligent to oversee and control our emotions. It can be useful to find a way to guarantee that you stay solid. These include:

- Taking Exercise and Keep Fit.

The hormones that we discharge when we are furious—mostly cortisol and adrenaline—are like those created when we are focused. At the point when you practice consistently, your body figures out how to control your adrenaline and cortisol levels more adequately. Individuals who are truly fit also have ideal degrees of endorphins, the hormones that cause you to feel great and more averse to feel irate.

- Resting soundly.

Rest is a significant piece of life and a great quality of rest can help battle numerous physical, mental, and emotional issues, including anger. At the point when we rest, the body and psyche rest and remake harmed cells and neural pathways. We all realize that individuals regularly feel better following a decent night's rest. The ideal degree of good quality rest is around seven hours per night, even though everyone is extraordinary and you may require more than this.

- Figure Out How to Manage Your Stress Levels.

Being under pressure makes it a lot harder to oversee emotions. It merits taking a look at your feelings of anxiety, and check whether you can lessen them by any means.

CHAPTER 11

REFLECTIVE PRACTICES

What is Reflective Practice? Reflective practice is, in its least complex structure, considering or thinking about what you do. It is firmly connected to the idea of gaining what you did, and what occurred and choose from that what you would do any other way next time.

Considering what has happened is a piece of being human. The distinction between easygoing 'thinking' and 'reflective practice' is that reflective practice requires a cognizant exertion to consider occasions, and form bits of knowledge into them. When you start utilizing reflective practice, you will think that its valuable both at work and at home.

Reflective Practice as a Skill

Reflective practice is an active, dynamic action-based and ethical set of skills, placed in real-time, and dealing with real, complex, and difficult situations.

Reflective practice is, in its simplest form, thinking about or reflecting on what you do. It is closely linked to the concept of learning from experience, in that you think about what you did, and what happened and decide from that what you would do differently next time.

Scholastics will concur that reflective practice overcomes any issues between the 'high ground' of hypothesis and the 'marshy swamps' of practice. As it were, it encourages us to investigate speculations and to apply them to our encounters in a progressively organized manner. These can either be formal hypotheses from scholastic research or from your very own thoughts. It also urges us to investigate our convictions and suspicions and to discover answers for issues.

Reflective practice is an aptitude that can be learned and sharpened, which is uplifting news for the majority of us.

Creating and Using Reflective Practice
What should be possible to help build up the basic, valuable, and inventive reasoning that is vital for reflective practice?

Neil Thompson, in his book *People Skills*, recommends that there are six stages:

- Peruse around the subjects you are finding out about or need to find out about and create.

- Get some information about how they get things done and why.

- Watch: what is happening around you.

- Feel: focus on your emotions, what prompts them, and how you manage negative ones.

- Talk: share your perspectives and encounters with others in your association.

- Think: figure out how to esteem time spent pondering your work.

As it were, it's not simply the reasoning that is significant. You also need to build up a comprehension of the hypothesis and other people's practice as well and investigate thoughts with others.

Reflective practice can be a mutual movement: it doesn't need to be done alone. In reality, some social analysts have proposed that learning possibly happens when thought is placed into language; either composed or spoken. This may clarify why we are persuaded to report a specific understanding so anyone can hear without anyone else around! It also has suggestions for reflective practice and implies that contemplations aren't unmistakably verbalized.

It tends to be hard to track down open doors for sharing a reflective practice in a bustling working environment. There are some undeniable ones, for example, evaluation meetings, or surveys of specific occasions, yet they don't occur each day. You have to discover different methods for articulating experiences.

Although it can feel somewhat devised, it very well may be useful—particularly from the start—to keep a diary of learning encounters. This isn't tied in with archiving formal courses, however, taking regular exercises and occasions, and recording what occurred, allows you to consider what you have gained from them, and what you could or ought to have done any other way. It's not just about changing: a learning diary and reflective practice can also feature when you've accomplished something well.

In your learning diary, it might be useful to work through a basic procedure. When you become progressively experienced, you will find that you need to join steps or move them around, yet this is probably going to be a decent beginning stage.

The Reflective Learning Process

Recognize a circumstance you experienced in your work or individual life that you accept that could have been managed better.

- Portray the experience

What was the deal? When and where did the circumstance happen? Are there any other contemplations you have about the circumstance?

- Reflection

How could you carry on? What contemplations did you have? How did it cause you to feel? Were there different components that impacted the circumstance? What have you gained from the experience?

- Conjecturing

How did the experience coordinate with your assumptions, for example, was the result expected or startling? How can it identify with any conventional speculations that you know? What practices do you think may have changed the result?

- Experimentation

Is there anything you could do or say presently to change the result? What action(s) would you be able to take to change comparable responses later on? What practices may you try out?

The Benefits of Reflective Practice

Reflective practice has gigantic advantages in expanding self-mindfulness, which is a key part of emotional insight, and in building up a superior comprehension of others. Reflective practice can also assist you with developing inventive reasoning aptitudes, and empowers dynamic commitment in work forms.

In work circumstances, keeping a learning diary, and routinely utilizing reflective practice, will bolster significant conversations about vocation improvement, and your self-improvement, including your individual evaluation time. It will also assist with furnishing you with guides to use in competency-based meeting circumstances.

- Caution.

Reflective practice is perhaps the simplest thing to drop when the weight is on, yet it's something that you would at least be able to stand to drop, particularly under those conditions. Time spent on reflective practice will guarantee that you are concentrating on the things that truly matter, both to you and to your boss or family.

To conclude: reflective practice is a technique for improving your learning both as an understudy and according to your work and educational encounters. Although it will require some investment to receive the method of reflective practice, it will also spare you time and energy.

CHAPTER 12
STRESS AND HOW TO MANAGE IT

Stress, as many people comprehend the term, is a response to over-abundant pressure. This may originate from life occasions, work, or essentially a sentiment of being somewhat crazy. By far most individuals will experience the ill effects of stress in any event in their lives, and many live with it a great part of the time.

Sadly, a lot of stress can be extremely terrible for your well-being, causing long haul issues like hypertension and heart conditions. This page gives a prologue to stress and clarifies a portion of its most regular causes and the side effects that you may see.

Characterizing Stress

The word reference definition of stress incorporates hardship, strain, physical, emotional, or mental weight.

It is a reaction to pressure and the improper significant level of weight.

Stress can be depicted as the distress that is caused because of requests set on physical or mental vitality. Stress regularly influences conduct, with the goal that stress in one individual is also prone to put stress on people around them, regardless of who family, companions, or partners are.

Various individuals find various things stressful, and can also adapt to various degrees of weight before getting stressed.

For instance, a few people think that it's stressful to be among enormous quantities of individuals and they keep away from swarms. Others like nothing but the possibility of a concert, with many individuals near one another for a couple of days. A few people find an excess of work stressful, while numerous others would state that it is stressful not to have enough to do.

It is in this way essential to recollect that stress is close to home, and don't judge others by all accounts of stressfulness.

Reasons for Stress

Stress can emerge as the aftereffect of various components, including life occasions, work, and conduct of others.

These will shift for various individuals, even though there are probably going to be some that we would all concur are stressful like losing your activity, isolating from your accomplice, and moving to another house.

Stressful Life Situations
A large number of the most stressful circumstances in life come because of impromptu changes close to home situations. There is some proof that what is stressful isn't so much the occasion itself, as the sentiment of being wild in your own life.

The accompanying rundown is ordered from the appropriate responses given by countless individuals concerning that it is so difficult to straighten out to various extraordinary occasions. A high score shows that individuals think that its difficult to straighten out to that occasion, which also demonstrates a high-stress factor.

Event:	Score out of 100
Demise of a Spouse or Partner:	100
Divorce:	73
Conjugal Separation:	65
Demise of a Close Family Member:	63
Individual Injury or Illness:	53
Marriage:	50
Loss of a Job:	47
Conjugal Reconciliation:	45
Retirement:	45
Change in Health of a Family Member:	44
Pregnancy:	40
Sexual Problems:	39
Expansion of a New Family Member:	39
Demise of a Close Friend:	37
Change to a Different Kind of Work:	36
Taking on a Large Mortgage:	31
Change of Responsibilities at Work:	29
Child or Daughter Leaving Home:	29
Life partner Starts or Stops Work:	26
Beginning or Leaving School:	26
Issue With the Boss:	23
Change in Residence:	20
Taking on a Loan:	17
Change in Eating Habits:	15
Holiday:	13
Christmas:	12
Minor Violations of the Law:	11

In light of Holmes and Rahe's Life Change Index; Journal of Psychosomatic Research, 1967, Vol. 11, pp. 213-218.

Life changes can directly affect well-being, either fortunate or unfortunate. Individuals who have high-stress life change regularly and become sick a short time later. Many people consider that the passing of a companion is the most stressful change throughout everyday life. Single men are 40% bound to bite the dust than others, and have high paces of ailment and melancholy.

It isn't just upsetting occasions that can be stressful. Practically any adjustment in conditions can cause stress as we straighten out. If conceivable, it is savvy to not have such a large number of changes in life happening all at once.

Certain circumstances can also prompt individuals feeling stressed, even though the level of stress will depend on that person's adapting systems.

The earth can make us stressed: for instance, clamor, swarms, poor lighting, contamination or other outside components over which we have no control can make us feel on edge and crabby.

Changing under cutting edge life can also be a wellspring of stress. We speak with individuals from numerous points of view like through the Internet, cell phones, and different communication media. The desire for a fast reaction has expanded.

We also have a lot more products accessible to us and a few people feel the desire to keep up a specific way of life and level of industrialism. Also, numerous individuals are both working and thinking about children or potentially more established guardians. Every one of these progressions implies that stress is tragically typical in both our own and professional lives.

Stress at Work
One specific condition where numerous individuals experience stress is grinding away.

Stress at work might be the aftereffect of being asked or expected to do excessively or work for extremely extended periods. It can also be the aftereffect of not being given enough work, or not having any comprehension of what is normal.

Also, with any type of stress, the root issue is regularly the inclination of not being in charge.

Signs and Symptoms of Stress

There are various basic signs and indications of stress, and stress can also prompt major issues and ailments.

Anxiety

Anxiety is caused when life occasions are felt to be threatening to individual physical, social, or mental well-being. The measure of anxiety experienced by an individual relies upon:

How compromising these life occasions are seen to be;

Singular adapting methodologies; and what number of stressful occasions happen in a brief time frame.

Anxiety is very common, and many people become on edge every once in a while. Nonetheless, anxiety can turn into an issue if it influences your capacity to deal with your life or manage the things that are causing your anxiety.

Pressure

Pressure is a characteristic response to anxiety or stress. It is a piece of crude endurance where physiological changes set up the person for 'fight or flight' through the arrival of the hormone adrenaline.

This thoughtful reaction, as it is known, brings about a substance called adenosine triphosphate (ATP) being discharged into the body and makes muscle tense good to go. Because of the adrenaline, the veins close to the skin choke to slow draining if the injury is continued and to expand the blood gracefully to the muscles, heart, lungs, and cerebrum. Assimilation is restrained, the bladder unwinds, the pulse and breathing rate increment, the body sweats more. You become more alert, your eyes enlarge, and you get a flood of vitality.

These reactions are very helpful in circumstances of physical danger like when you are being pursued by a wild creature.

Be that as it may, for the greater part of us these days, tensions can't be settled by a 'fight or flight' response, or by any physical reaction.

Present-day stressful circumstances will proceed for any longer time frames. A quick reaction doesn't typically calm the anxiety-inciting circumstance. In this way, we wind up living in a drawn-out condition of anxiety, which can prompt the side effects regularly connected with stress. These keep people from unwinding and can be averse to well-being.

Physical Signs of Stress
Feeling uncomfortable, tense and stressed, physical impressions of proceeded stress can include:

- Palpitations.

- Wooziness.

- Acid reflux or indigestion.

- Strain migraines.

- Hurting muscles.

- Trembling or eye jerks.

- Looseness of the bowels.

- Sleep deprivation.

- Tiredness.

- Ineptitude.

Proceeded stress can prompt sentiments of dormancy and tiredness, headaches, serious stomach cramps, and restlessness. Extreme stress can also prompt fits of anxiety, chest agonies, and fears of being truly sick.

Similarly, as with every such manifestation, you should look for the assistance and guidance of a human services professional.

A key issue is to perceive that these side effects are brought about by stress. When this is clear, you can begin to make a move to deal with the causes and not simply the side effects.

This should be possible through learning various stress decrease procedures.

Avoiding and Managing Stress

Stress happens as a response to over the top pressure. It is described by feeling under pressure, or unfit to adapt. You may also have physical manifestations like cerebral pains, sweat-soaked palms, and a hustling heartbeat when you are stressed. A little stress isn't commonly viewed as unsafe, yet a lot of extensive stretching can affect your well-being.

It is critical to figure out how to oversee stress. This remembers both figuring out how to abstain from getting stressed for the primary spot and taking activities to diminish stress when it happens. This page talks about both these issues and recommends some straightforward and further developed manners which can help you to maintain a strategic distance from stress and decrease your stress in life.

Perceiving Stress

The initial phase in keeping away from or lessening stress is to perceive when you are stressed.

There are various basic signs or side effects of stress. In any case, not every person will encounter them all every time they are stressed. Others may find that they have different signs: for instance, feeling exceptionally tearful or over-emotional. It is useful to know about your 'stress signs' with the goal that you know when you are getting stressed and you can take care of business.

The following stage is to comprehend your 'triggers': the occasions, individuals, or conditions that cause you to get stressed.

Everybody has various things that cause them to feel stressed. Some might be present in the moment, for example, being in a group—and others might be longer-term, for example, a relationship breakdown, or an issue with an associate at work. When you comprehend what is making you stressed, at that point you can begin to address the causes.

Top Tip!

Keep a Stress Diary

It tends to be useful to keep a 'stress journal'. Every day for half a month, monitor the things you have done, individuals you have met, and how you have felt.

This will assist you in identifying circumstances that have made you feel stressed.

Overseeing Stress
There are two primary methodologies to overseeing stress: evasion and decrease. A third option is to figure out how to live with it, yet this is most likely not a drawn-out arrangement on the impacts on your well-being.

Maintaining a Strategic Distance from Stress
Maintaining a strategic distance from stress involves not placing yourself in stressful circumstances.

This sounds sufficiently straightforward—and at times, it might. For instance, if you discover traffic jams are stressful, you may decide not to drive to work by car. Or you can arrange a prior or later starting work-time or directly working from home.

It might be difficult to deal with certain circumstances. There are various things you can do, but to make it simpler to maintain a strategic distance from stressful circumstances is vital. These include:

- Being set up to say no.

For some individuals, 'no' is perhaps the hardest word to state. From the time we are little kids, we are instructed that idiom 'no' is discourteous, that people don't care for it. Be that as it may, figuring out how to state 'no' is a fundamental method to shield yourself from abundance stress.

- Knowing your cutoff points and being set up to concede rout.

You don't need to take care of each issue on the planet. Nor do you need to stay with a circumstance until it makes you sick. Now and again the most ideal approach to take care of an issue is to forsake it. It might want to be vanquished to change your activity since you can't adapt to the requests that it is putting on you. Once in a while, getting another line of work is simpler than changing your work environment. Know your cutoff points.

- Figuring out how to disparage what can be accomplished.

Individuals overestimate their capacities and what they can accomplish in a given time. Start thinking little of what can be accomplished and give yourself additional time. People will be far more joyful if you guarantee less and convey more than the other way around.

- Being set up to make changes to your life.

To expel yourself from stressful circumstances may require you to roll out certain improvements throughout your life—which may, in itself, be characteristically stressful. In any case, it merits considering whether you are set up to do this if you can't stay away from or oversee stress by some other methods.

Overseeing and Minimizing Stress
The subsequent fundamental way to deal with overseeing stress is to lessen the level that you experience or the impact that it has on you.

There are various ways you can do that.

1. Take Care of Yourself Appropriately

Individuals are better ready to adapt to stress when their bodies are sound.

This is mostly because when you are fit and well, you can basically adapt because unforeseen weakness is a significant wellspring of stress.

There are three principle zones to see: diet, exercise, and rest.

Setting aside a few minutes for physical exercise in your standard routine will assist with improving muscle control, cause you to feel more beneficial, and build self-esteem. You may feel that you don't have time, however, the advantages will more than reimburse the thirty minutes or so away from your plan for the day.

Attempt to improve your eating regimen and maintain a strategic distance from energizers as much as possible could help. Overabundance of caffeine or nicotine can cause people to feel on edge or anxious. It tends to be enticing to go to a lousy nourishment to spare time, yet it won't help you in the long haul. Setting aside an effort to prepare dinner, regardless of whether it is just something straightforward, is useful in soothing stress since it causes you to feel that you are caring for yourself.

You also need to guarantee that you get enough rest. Try not to attempt to work or do things until you wish to fall into bed. Rather, take thirty minutes or so before you hit the hay to loosen up a little. Doing some physical exercise can also assist you with sleeping better since it implies your body is worn out. The same can also be said for your psyche.

2. Work to Unwind and Have a Fabulous Time

Numerous individuals do exclude unwinding or 'fun' time in their calendars, yet both are critical for diminishing stress.

Cognizant unwinding is significant for your body and mind, which can assist you in managing the negatives of stress. An extremely wide scope of unwinding strategies have been created, albeit many can be viewed as a minor departure from various fundamental techniques. They will spotlight on either the physical sentiments of pressure or utilize mental symbolism to initiate silence and tranquility.

Maybe the most impressive strategy for unwinding is care. At its most straightforward, care is concentrating on the present second, the present time and place, and permitting—through a kind of meditation—stress over the future or laments about the past to dissolve away. Nonetheless, it is also a generally excellent procedure to diminish stress, and you may jump at the chance to peruse our visitor post on overseeing stress with care to find out additional information.

It can also be useful to design time into your calendar to accomplish something that you appreciate. If this is a physical exercise, it might even tick two boxes!

Anticipating the occasions when you can accomplish something that gives you joy will help when you need to adapt to less lovely parts of life. You may need to accomplish some work on your time management to assist you with making more time. However, it will be well justified despite all the trouble.

3. Think Positively

Your brain is an extremely amazing thing. It can drag you down and it can also develop you.

At the point when we are stressed, it is enticing to concentrate on everything difficult, or what is turning out badly in our lives. Be that as it may, suspecting more positively—for instance, by seeing what has gone well that day or week, or considerably over a more extended period—can affect your state of mind.

It is worth deliberately abstaining from dwelling on any disappointments and ensuring that you reward yourself for your victories. You have to acknowledge that everybody has restrictions and can't prevail at everything, and think about what you have accomplished.

4. Look for Help from Others
Try not to feel that you need to adapt to your issues alone.

Requesting help is regularly hard, however, it is an excellent initial move towards dealing with your stress better.

Having somebody to share your issues can significantly assist with offloading stress. You may think that it's valuable to converse with a companion or work associate. You can also converse with your line chief or business if you're encountering stress in the work environment.

- It's okay not to be okay.

- Not every person can deal with their stress levels or oversee them constantly.

- It is okay to feel like you can't adapt.

Be that as it may, it isn't okay to feel that you have to prop up in any case.

If you are stressed over your stress levels or are attempting to oversee or maintain a strategic distance from stress, at that point it is significant that you request help. In the primary occasion, you may address or confide in a companion or associate, yet it is also a smart thought to address your PCP or other human services supplier.

A few people find that they need a drug to help mitigate the side effects of stress.

Drugs might be recommended to treat the prompt manifestations of stress or to assist somebody with getting through an emergency. It won't address the reasons for stress in the long haul, so you ought to also consider how to address those. Medicine may also prompt reliance, so if you think you need drugs to help with your stress, you ought to examine your choices cautiously with your PCP or other human services supplier.

You ought to also address your primary care physician if you figure you might be discouraged. Wretchedness is a genuine ailment yet it is normal and treatable.

Numerous individuals also utilize corresponding and elective treatments to assist with controlling stress.

There are numerous treatments used to manage stress, including:

- Alexander Procedure

- Aromatherapy

- Self-Hypnosis

- Massage

- Mindful Meditation

- Yoga

- Tai chi

- Music therapy

- Laughter therapy

In summary, many people experience the ill effects of stress sooner or later in their lives. A comprehension of the reasons for stress and figuring out how to stay away from stressful circumstances will help ease a portion of its negative outcomes.

A few people may also think that its valuable to utilize prescription or an integral treatment, or some type of self-help identified with unwinding to help deal with their stress.

CHAPTER 13

MINDFULNESS

What is mindfulness? Set forth plainly, mindfulness is attention to the current moment and situation.

The idea of mindfulness is of Buddhist origin and can be characterized from various perspectives in current society: for instance, as a sort of mental disposition that one may receive, or a lot of strategies that can stay in an individual's cognizance in the present.

Individuals think of numerous considerations immediately and a significant number of them are worried about the past, or the future, or conceptual things.

Being mindful means keeping your brain at the present time and place. This can be very quieting, permitting stresses and laments to be disregarded, particularly when it is the focal point of meditation.

Mindfulness is oftentimes talked about in the media as a treatment for some things, including genuine anxiety and despondency, ceaseless torment, and sentiments of being overpowered by present-day life, stress help.

Be that as it may, being mindful isn't in every case simple, and mindful meditation specifically needs standard practice to get a hang of it.

How Mindfulness Became Fashionable

Jon Kabat-Zinn is an American atomic scholar who was acquainted with Buddhism as an understudy and understood that the idea of mindfulness could have massive uses in decreasing stress.

He built up a course called Mindfulness-Based Stress Reduction (MBSR) at the University of Massachusetts and became known world-wide after his first book, Full Catastrophe Living: Using the Wisdom of Your Body and Mind to Face Stress, Pain, and Illness (Delta, 1991), was distributed.

His program broadly incorporated an activity-dependent on eating a raisin: an extremely basic assignment yet performed with exceptional concentration and focus that sets regardless of different considerations.

How might I be 'Mindful?'
One may decide to be mindful in day by day life essentially by focusing on current undertakings. However, mindfulness is normally connected with doing as such with a specific mentality of interest, transparency, and acknowledgment. That way you can be available to your genuine encounter, liberated from assumptions, and without being occupied by your responses to it.

Mindfulness is at its most intense when one is focusing on one's brain completely on such a condition of mental centers being depicted as meditation. Meditation is in some cases is portrayed as 'falling conscious' as a difference to nodding off.

Meditation can be delegated fixation intervention, where there is one specific center, for example, a sound, or as mindfulness meditation where the attention is on all parts of the current second.

In any case, total consciousness of the present is simpler to accomplish by giving specific consideration to one part of it, at any rate at first, so the two sorts of meditation are interwoven.

The development of breath into and out of the body is an extremely well known introductory focal point of consideration in mindful meditation as it is constantly present and includes simply enough real development to keep one intrigued.

A few people favor a rehashed quiet expression (called a mantra), or a lot of musical, basic developments, or appreciate being guided through a meditation by verbal directions and updates from an instructor or a soundtrack. Many guided meditations are accessible on the web and there are also various applications that are promptly accessible. Numerous religions utilize reflective states as an instrument, from the thoughts of Christian priests and nuns to the spinning dervishes found inside pieces of Islam. In any case, the practice of meditation can also be mainstream. For the most part, individuals sit discreetly on an upstanding seat with the goal that they are loose however alert. You can ruminate resting, sitting on a transport or in any event, strolling.

What Would Mindfulness Be Helpful For?

The physical and psychological expression that mindfulness achieves can be useful in treating numerous sicknesses since stress is a key factor in everything from coronary illness to bipolar turmoil.

Mindfulness also helps numerous individuals who are not 'sick', however, they feel that they could be carrying on a more joyful and progressively important life.

In any case, there are two specific conditions that mindfulness can have a specific effect upon:

1. Sorrow
At the point when we are discouraged, our negative contemplations and negative temperaments become interwoven.

We feel dreadful, we think we are a horrendous individual or that everything will be terrible, and that aggravates our state of mind even more. A downwards winding is exceptionally simple to get into, particularly if you have been discouraged previously, and we gain no joy from the things that generally cheer us up, and nor would we be able to see anything in context.

Mindfulness assists with ending the heightening of the negative considerations related to misery and instructs us to concentrate on the current second, as opposed to remembering the past or being worried about what's to come.

Mindfulness can assist us with encountering the world legitimately and without judgment. We may see that we are feeling terrible, however, we acknowledge it instead of attempting to battle it, or let it stress us, and we don't freeze. Ideally, a discouraged state can be stayed away from along these lines or at any rate acknowledged: individuals with misery feel remorseful or on edge about being discouraged and that aggravates it.

These methods are called Mindfulness-Based Cognitive Therapy or MBCT.

2. Incessant Pain

Individuals who are in incessant agony have stuck there because their cerebrum became receptive to torment during a unique difficult condition.

In this way, although they are mended from a physical point of view, their cerebrums are so well wired to feel torment that they take a great deal of persuading that the body isn't—truth be told—under any danger.

Victims are normally caught in a cycle where they have a decent day, do excessively, and afterward have a terrible day or a few of them, doing a process known as movement cycling.

The 're-wiring' of the mind required is normally done by the victim remaining well inside their cutoff points and afterward, step by step expanding their degree of action. Incomprehensibly, it is also imperative to practice the body tenderly with the goal that the mind quits 'fearing' certain regions.

Victims, as a rule, endeavor to hold a difficult region inflexibly with the goal that it never moves, and the held muscles that outcomes can be worthwhile motivation for more torment!

Mindfulness implies that the victim is mindful of their agony, and afterward acknowledges it, instead of stressing that they are harming and not going to have the option to accomplish something later on.

It also implies that they barely know when they have to rest and don't drive themselves too hard, and consequently maintain a strategic distance from action cycling. This procedure isn't simple and incessant agony programs don't bring about a total non-attendance of torment.

In any case, victims find that they deal with their agony much better and appreciate life undeniably more. Vidyamala Burch has composed broadly regarding this matter and her 'Breath works' programs, which depends vigorously on mindfulness, have helped a large number of individuals.

Many organizations, such as companies, hospitals, and schools, are getting more aware of the fact that mindfulness training is of great help to their employees and their clients. You can attempt experiencing the multitude of benefits of mindfulness on your own just by taking a few quiet minutes to breathe slowly and observe little details around you.

Science of Mindfulness – 3 Ways to Get the Benefits of Meditation

If one thing's been experimentally demonstrated to improve the life quality of an individual, it's mindfulness.

Research has demonstrated that mindfulness:

- Diminishes stress.

- It can treat anxiety and sadness as viably as antidepressants.

- Improves resolve.

- Expands the thickness of the dim issue in your mind.

Believe it or not, mindfulness doesn't simply improve your abstract well-being, it truly changes the piece of your cerebrum that is related to stress-decrease as well.

What Is Mindfulness?

Is mindfulness something you get when you live in a surrender and mull over the idea of presence? Is it something you find by meeting an otherworldly master at the highest point of a forlorn mountain? Not really.

Mindfulness is the inclination you get when you lose all sense of direction in somebody's eyes (or lost in sixteen ounces of Cherry Garcia frozen yogurt), and you become completely invested in the tactile experience.

We invest a large portion of our energy contemplating the past or the future, however, mindfulness is a condition of inundation right now.

The human mind is intended to continually pass judgment. Considerations go through our head like:

"For what reason do I feel so worn out?"

"What would I be able to do to dispose of this stress I'm feeling?"

"For what reason did I eat an entire sixteen ounces of Cherry Garcia at a time?"

Mindfulness is a state wherein your awareness no longer burns through effort on judging. This liberates it to concentrate totally on encountering.

Mindfulness is incredible. For a considerable lot of us, our best recollections are minutes, which we encounter at a high level of mindfulness.

Anybody can prepare their psyche to get mindful. Be that as it may, our endeavors to do so are regularly destined from the beginning due to two inescapable social myths about mindfulness.

Myth 1: Mindfulness Is Religious
Mindfulness is emphatically connected with eastern profound customs. At the point when we consider mindfulness, we consider Chakra arrangement and priests who've surrendered all their physical belongings. Also, mindfulness can be attached to a strict practice, however, in no way, shape, or form should be.

Meditation is the most well-known strategy for bringing more mindfulness into your life. Meditation isn't strict, it is essentially a technique for preparing the brain, like how exercise prepares the body.

Mindfulness meditation is the practice of getting mindful of your musings and emotions. The more you contemplate, the more regularly you'll have the option to get to a condition of mindfulness. (regardless of whether you don't surrender every one of your assets and join a religious community.)

Myth 2: Mindfulness Is Emptying Your Mind of Thought
The most across the board myth about mindfulness is also the most hazardous. Mindfulness is frequently thought of as an approach to control your considerations.

Mindfulness isn't tied in with killing the voice in your mind; that would be an unthinkable undertaking. Attempting to control the brain just upsets it to turn out to be progressively hyperactive.

Do you realize those Chinese finger traps where you put every one of your pointers in a single side? The harder you attempt to pull your fingers from one another, the more tightly the snare holds you. That is the thing that attempts to control your considerations.

Chinese finger traps have a nonsensical arrangement. Rather than pulling your fingers from one another, you push them towards one another, and the snare slackens its hold. That is the thing that mindfulness resembles. It's not tied in with battling against your contemplations, it's tied in with figuring out how to acknowledge them as they seem to be. You can't constrain mindfulness by attempting to control your musings, you slide into it delicately by getting mindful of your considerations.

Numerous individuals attempt meditation once and surrender since it's disappointing that they can't kill their brains for more than several seconds.

Be that as it may, the objective of meditation isn't to clear the psyche. It's attempting to clear the brain with how it has something contrary to the planned impact.

If you somehow managed to lift loads once, you wouldn't hope to look like Thor before an hour's over meeting. Correspondingly, there's no motivation to be disappointed if rehearsing mindfulness doesn't void your psyche of all ideas. That isn't the objective of mindfulness in any case.

Benefits of Meditation in a World Addicted to Distraction
In the cutting-edge world, our psyches are prepared by innovation to be in a steady condition of interruption. Presently, like never before, finding a way to construct mindfulness has huge advantages.

The way of thinking supporting this culture of interruption is that our general surroundings are uninteresting and, to feel better, we should discover something more captivating to do. (like reviving Instagram at regular intervals.)

The way of thinking supporting mindfulness is the inverse: the world around is a dining experience for the faculties holding back to be delighted in and, by figuring out how to surrender the craving to be elsewhere, we can completely inundate ourselves right now.

Step By Step Instructions to Get the Benefits of Meditation in Your Life

All in all, mindfulness can essentially improve the nature of our lives, yet how would we get a greater amount of it? Committed practice.

Presently, meditation is one course to mindfulness, however, it's not by any means the only alternative. There are three strategies for practicing mindfulness that are especially powerful.

1. Mindful Strolling
Mindful strolling is a technique that carries thoughtful practice into the outside world. Rather than sitting in a calm room, you're investigating nature.

Mindful strolling permits you to take out two targets with one shot. Not exclusively will you gain the stress-decrease advantages of meditation, yet strolling can also be a shockingly successful type of activity for improving your well-being and getting more fit.

For a stroll to be a mindfulness practice, your goal ought to be to see both your contemplations and your general surroundings. As you walk, try to take in the fragrances, to feel the breeze on your skin. (or if like me, you live in Arizona, feel the sun consuming your skin.) Truly take in the sights, the sounds, and the sentiments you experience.

Above all, notice when you get diverted. As musings go through your head about what you need to do later, or you begin deciding your experience (for example "It's excessively hot", or "When did I become a flower child who goes on mindful strolls?") notice those musings. The objective isn't to dispose of your contemplations, it's simply to be aware of them. The piece of your psyche that you get to when you notice your reasoning, that is mindfulness. By tuning into that piece of your brain during your walk, you are fortifying your capacity to pick up the advantages of meditation while on your walk for the day. (PS: It's best practice to leave your telephone at home, or at any rate, to kill notifications and keep it in your pocket during your mindful walk.)

2. Yoga

In the west, yoga is observed as a kind of activity, but on the other hand, it's an extraordinary strategy for rehearsing mindfulness. While doing yoga, you can concentrate on the sensations in your body just as the contemplations are experiencing it in your brain.

During yoga, you can hope to feel a modest quantity of physical uneasiness as you stretch your body past its typical cutoff points. This uneasiness is an open door for preparing your body, yet your psyche too. Try not to keep away from the agony, let it in, acknowledge it as it is—doing so will assist you with bringing mindfulness into your day to day life.

Although yoga is the type of activity most connected with mindfulness, you can transform any kind of solo exercise into a reflective encounter.

Regardless of whether you're weightlifting, running, biking, or shooting free-tosses, you can practice carrying your attention to the subtleties of what you're doing: the inclination of your legs hitting the asphalt, the pressure in your arms as you push a substantial weight, or seeing a b-ball traveling through the air. (and in case you're similar to me, seeing the ball miss the bushel by around two feet.)

For exercise to be a type of devoted mindfulness preparation, it's best done alone because interfacing with others will make it hard to concentrate on your psychological practice.

3. Meditation

There are various kinds of meditation you can practice. Here, we're going to concentrate on mindfulness meditation, which is the thing that most mental research has concentrated on.

To begin, sit down with your back straight. It's ideal to abstain from setting down because that can transform your meditation into a greater extent of a snooze. You don't need to sit on the floor; you can sit on a seat, against a love seat, or any way you like.

At the point when you're first beginning, I suggest keeping your practice meetings generally short (from five to fifteen minutes). It'll be simpler to gather speed and keep up meditation as long-haul propensity that way.

While sitting, basically watch your breath. You can concentrate on broadcasting live traveling through your nose and mouth. You can see the extension of your lungs. Or, on the other hand, you can focus on any of the different sensations you feel while relaxing. As you do this, you will undoubtedly begin to float off. Your psyche will consider everything other than your breath. As this occurs, don't get disappointed or feel like you're doing meditation wrong. Simply recognize that you floated off and take your consideration back to the breath.

You don't need to attempt to stop your contemplations, essentially try to see when you get enveloped with them. Keep in mind, the piece of your awareness that sees when you lose all sense of direction in thought, is mindfulness.

An elective strategy for rehearsing mindfulness is to concentrate on your breath, yet on any of your faculties. Focus on the sounds in the room and outside, the sensations on your skin, and so forth. Attempt the two techniques and utilize whatever resonates most with you.

In a ten minute meditation meeting, you can hope to lose all sense of direction in considered times. That is alright. Keep in mind, hoping to be mindful of your breath for a few minutes resembles hoping to seat press 300 beats on your first outing to the rec center.

Your meditation will construct your mindfulness muscle. As many months pass by, you will gain the advantages of meditation during your practice for the day.

Guided Meditations
Guided meditations are valuable for a similar explanation that taking music exercises is useful. In case you're beginning to get familiar with the guitar, the trouble of the underlying learning time frame can be both disappointing and demoralizing. A decent instructor can point you the correct way and help right the slip-ups you're making.

With mindfulness, utilizing guided meditation as a learning device can assist you with feeling certain that you're 'doing it right,' and it can quicken your underlying expectation to learn and adapt.

There is a large number of guided meditations you can discover online through Google or YouTube. My undisputed top choices are the applications Calm and Headspace, the two of which have a fledgling arrangement to give you the general tour of meditation. The sites Tarabrach.com and the UCLA Mindfulness Research Center also have top-notch free guided meditations you can look at.

Given a portion of our most famous substance, this book will assist you with living a more joyful, more beneficial, and progressively gainful life.

Mindfulness may appear as though a craze saved for 'granola crunchers', yet logical investigations have given broad proof to the advantages of reflective practices.

Moreover, renowned creators of Tools of Titans, Tim Ferris has interviewed more than 200 world-class performers (on-screen characters, businessmen, competitors) about their tools and tactics. Tim Ferris saw that one of the most widely recognized tools for exceptionally effective individuals is some kind of thoughtful practice. Mindfulness permits us to get away from the futile way of life and to genuinely encounter the lavishness encompassing us at any second.

The greater part of us invests our energy and satisfaction on something we'll gain when we arrive at an objective or get an advancement. Mindfulness is an alternate methodology. Rather than attempting to make bliss, it's tied in with finding the joy that is accessible to us at this moment, right now.

Seven Mindfulness Pillars to Build Self-Esteem

It's an obvious fact that a ton of what we think and do are the results of our propensities. These propensities are frequently completed unwittingly and they lead to our emotions and convictions. These emotions and convictions at that point lead to specific activities. These activities can strengthen our convictions or have results that begin the cycle once more.

As a rule, mindfulness has two significant perspectives on it.

The first includes the accompanying:

- Being commonly mindful of the current second.

- Noticing when that mindfulness meanders.

- Bringing that mindfulness back to the current second.

The second most normal part of mindfulness is concentrating on something specific. This includes:

- Paying regard for something specifically, similar to one's breath.

- Noticing when the brain floats from that thing.

- Bringing consideration back to that thing.

Reinforcing Mindfulness for Self-Esteem
Mindfulness is an ability that most Westerners are not used to. Turning out to be progressively mindful generally takes explicit types of practice. Numerous conventions and techniques have been created throughout the years.

The various types of meditation have been commonly acknowledged as a mindfulness practice. With all things considered, the fundamental objective of being progressively mindful is to apply its standards to genuine circumstances.

1. Remain in the Present Moment
The vast majority of your distressful sentiments are either recollections of things turned out badly or contemplations of a not ideal future. If you end up feeling less certain, chances are you've been bothering past disappointments or are stressing over a specific result.

You should endeavor to cautiously see when your psyche isn't centered around the present. At the point when you notice your mindfulness floating, take it back to the present time and place. Focus on what you're doing well right now. As the older-timers say, "If you've got one foot in tomorrow and one foot in yesterday, you're pissing all over today."

Try not to befuddle ruminating and stressing over the future with arranging. Contingent upon how instilled your propensity towards negative reasoning is, it very well may be a dainty line among stressing and arranging.

Consider it like this.

If you reveal to yourself that you will do x, y, and z, it's generally arranging. Be that as it may, if your believing is along the lines of 'imagine a scenario where' or 'such is most likely going to occur', at that point you're presumably stressing.

2. Try not to Pass Judgment
'Do not judge, or you will be judged'. This saying has more truth to it than what people figure out. Judging can turn into an impressive,

oblivious propensity. What you don't understand is that by deciding for others, you're drawing correlations.

You will judge somebody to be greater at something than you. What's more, when that occurs, you will begin to down yourself and assault your self-esteem.

A decent method to practice being non-critical is to watch the news or read the paper and not structure a sentiment about what you see. At the end of the day, do whatever it takes not to feel that the occasion, the individuals in question, or their activities are correct, off-base, brilliant or inept, and so forth. At that point, attempt to carry this equivalent outlook when managing others.

At the point when you judge others, your brain sneaks out of the current second. It makes you defenseless against ruminating about the past and future. Keep in mind, judge not, or so you will be judged.

3. Stand Tall
Research has demonstrated that remaining with a great stance can effectively affect your temperament. It is difficult to stroll with one's head, shoulders, and chest held upstanding and not feel better. In case you're remaining with an acceptable stance, the vast majority will take a look at you and treat you as though you are certain. It can assist you with resting easy thinking about yourself.

One of the blocks that make it hard for some individuals with low self-worth to stand tall is dread of eye to eye connection. If you remember the two past advances, remaining in the present and shaping no decisions will be simpler for you to look at individuals without flinching.

Try not to gaze. Just ever so often look at individuals without flinching, particularly if they're taking a look at you. If you discover eye to eye connection is hard, there are a few hacks for it. You can take a look at the extension of an individual's nose, rather than legitimately in the eye. Another stunt is to take a look at an individual's ears in case you're not close to them.

4. Request Your Space
Individuals with low self-esteem regularly would prefer not to be taken note. When out in the open, they attempt to be as unpretentious as could reasonably be expected. Even though individuals with high self-worth stick out, one of the manners they do this is by occupying the room.

For example, when standing, attempt to keep your feet and shoulder-width separated. When sitting, keep your knees separated as much as is proper for the circumstance. At the point when you do this, you're fundamentally telling the world that you have balls, however, they're enormous ones. Attempt to get your hands far from you too, being mindful not to reliably overlay your arms over your chest.

5. Make Faces
The look of you hanging over regularly impacts your state of mind. You ought to have the appearance of a sure champ. Various individuals show that in an unexpected way.

For one individual, it could be a grinning face. For another, it could be the vibe of an individual who's not kidding and doesn't mess around. The decision is yours, as long as it is the outward appearance that you feel a certain individual would wear.

A lot of times, when you have low self-esteem, you rout yourself before you even beginning. You view thrashing, accommodation or misery all over it. In addition to the fact that this affects your state of mind, it can impact people around you too.

At the point when you grin, the entire world grins with you. If you look peppy and certain, it can make it simpler for individuals to float towards you. Individuals naturally realize that emotions are infectious. In this manner, people will be pulled in to individuals who feel better.

Then again, if you resemble a discouraged washout, not exclusively will you feel that way, yet it can make individuals unfriendly towards you. They would prefer not to feel like you do, so they will maintain a strategic distance from you or drive you away. You'll even discover individuals will regularly be pulled in towards you if you look slightly angry. The catchphrase is 'somewhat'. If you look goaded or prepared to detonate, individuals may watch out of dread for their physical well-being. Anger isn't commonly viewed as a positive emotion, however, a furious individual is looked at as having more confidence than one who looks agreeable.

6. Unwind
Unwinding methods help to mitigate the impacts of the fight or flight reaction. Being in a casual state won't manufacture confidence, however, it can assist with mitigating anxiety and other unfavorable dispositions. This progression takes practice.

First and foremost, it's suggested that you practice some sort of unwinding procedure. This is with the goal that you comprehend what unwinding feels like. When you have set up how it feels, you'll must be mindful of the stress on your body. The normal difficulty spots are the face, neck, shoulder, and the middle of your back. During your day, you can do a fast self-verification whether there is pointless tension in tough situation spots.

7. Go About as Though

This step incorporates bringing the various advances together. It's similar to being a technique on-screen character.

You mull over how you would envision an individual with high self-esteem would act and afterward you manage to copy that kind of conduct. It might be ungainly from the start and individuals that realize you might be put off a bit. They may not take the 'upgraded' version of yourself genuinely. Yet, in case you're predictable, they will fall in line. The key is consistency.

You will slip into your routine methods for carrying on. This is the place mindfulness has its impact. You need to prepare your psyche to get mindful of your musings, perspectives, and practices so you can address them at the earliest opportunity. Whenever done regularly and reliably enough, this will turn into a propensity.

We see that high self-worth can be affected by what you do and don't do. Continuously recollect that it's about advancement and not flawlessness. You ought to endeavor to be mindful of utilizing your musings and conduct to:

- Prevent self-crushing contemplations from emerging.

- Eliminate self-crushing contemplations that do emerge.

- Bring up esteem building contemplations when they are not at the top of the priority list.

- Maintain esteem building musings that are right now at the top of the priority list.

If you need moderate gains in your self-esteem, be mindful of the means you take to travel through life. Your cutoff points are just set by the restrictions of your mentality.

Seven Ways Mindfulness Can Unlock the Door to Your Authentic Life

"Numerous individuals are alive however don't contact the wonder of being alive."

— Thich Nhat Hanh, The Miracle of Mindfulness

In the middle of work, family, and web-based life, we take scarcely any valuable minutes to think about our lives and understand the significance of mindfulness.

Maybe, you deliberately abstained from taking a look at your life because, in case you're genuine, it very well may be severe. Simply consider the tidal wave of critical musings that overwhelmed your brain and caused you a lot of stress and anxiety.

As anyone might expect, a great deal of stress is only as a result of our general public. In any case, our more prominent individual disappointments are the consequence of our inner strife driven by disarray.

Is it true that you are feeling befuddled?

You're not alone. Notice how disarray is self-obvious everywhere throughout the world.

Research scientist Kathryn Tristan proposes in her book *Why Worry* that eventually in our lives, half of us in the U.S. will experience the ill effects of anxiety, despondency, or dependence—something contrary to a genuine life.

Be that as it may, at that point something mystic occurs.

On your path home from work or a surged supper out, the sunset's rising brilliant moon enraptures you and you experience a snapshot of joy and express harmony.

Everything is connected with the world and you weren't considering a thing. You were simply alive and splendidly so!

1. From Mundane to Extraordinary
What was the move?

The billows of disarray lifted. For a second, you were in flawless parity, intentionally mindful of the supernatural occurrence of life that includes you.

Here's the 10,000-foot view:

You were being your best, most real self as opposed to tuning in to constant, self-constraining idea designs.

Realness rises when you live from psyche and body, however, from the heart which is your normal state. Done deliberately, it is mindful living. It is the dominance of life.

An actual existence lived without a central core is a real existence loaded up with disarrays. This can show issues in your own life.

In his book, Living from the Heart, Nirmala stated, "what you are seeing, smelling, hearing, sensing, and pondering is limited by and filtered through your thoughts. Your thoughts mediate between you and reality and interfere with seeing it more fully and purely."

As indicated by neuroscience, what contemplations are and what offers to ascend to them is a secret.

Consider musings of one of the numerous valuable apparatuses the brain uses to explore our physical world. Without anyone else, contemplations are a two-dimensional brain wall.

Extended mindfulness that incorporates the heart implies a far more extravagant life that is satisfying and pays little heed to the conditions of what you are doing.

Stunning to a few, you don't need to do anything at all to encounter a valid life.

Be that as it may, ask yourself this:

Would you rather go through a meadow at sunset with a fence? Or, on the other hand, a meadow of your life unhindered to the extent the eye can see or even past that?

At the point when we live from the more comprehensive truth of our brain, body, and soul (heart), we open our lives to the extraordinary.

The most effective method to appreciate the marvel of your genuine life:

Slow life as the day progressed.

Although you're not completely mindful of the significance of mindfulness, you've been rehearsing it discontinuously for an incredible duration without acknowledging it. Submerging yourself in nature, taking a walk and even hand-washing dishes are types of mindfulness.

Review how you felt a feeling of quiet and well-being inside your body. Notice how adjusted your reality became. Presently, do these things intentionally and with your heart. Include yoga and meditation.

Life gets colossally fulfilling when we let go of our psychological desires and enter the 'Zen' of the stream.

2. Thoughts are linear
Attempting to solve thoughts with more thoughts was Einstein's definition of insanity. Move beyond whether the glass is half empty or half full, tapping into the external and internal spring of your highest wisdom instead.

At whatever point there's a challenge, rather than carelessly and impulsively reacting, surprise those involved by remaining silent. When we don't allow space around our thoughts, we are reactive rather than response-able.

Silence is incredibly amazing and contains miracles. It shifts, even breaks, routine patterns.

3. Quit Any Pretense of Getting Ready for 90 Days
In Western culture, arranging is believed to be the best resource. Google the intensity of arranging and you'll be immersed with reasons why an arrangement is central to arriving at your objectives.

It is safe to say that you will make the way for the significantly higher intensity of amalgamation that the Harvard Business Review calls 'key reasoning?'

Key reasoning relinquishes arranging at first, incorporating instinct and inventiveness to permit immediacy to show up normally.

Albert Einstein stated, "The instinctive psyche is a sacrosanct blessing and the discerning brain is a dedicated worker. We have made a general public that respects the hireling and has overlooked the blessing."

As opposed to anticipating various potential situations, be a clear record by asking, "What's straight away?"

Leaving a vast chance open is to make a vacuum that life must fill. It's more impressive than anticipating envisioned and favored situations which contain limits.

4. State "I Don't Have a Clue" Frequently
In any event to yourself!

Vacancy is exceptionally testing when you are compelled by society to fill each niche and corner with hecticness. Your brain will make certain to shout it at you with each possibility it gets. Vacancy expels all boundaries, including you escaping your specific manner.

I can let you know, given my experience as an essayist, that the dream is inside. Any craftsman or innovative individual will consent to that. All motivation emerges from the void of vacancy. Get settled with vacancy and figure out how to play with boundless prospects.

I for one lean toward being a clear record every opportunity I get. Like the informal Buddhist mantra says, "Vacant, unfilled. Cheerful, glad."

5. Open Yourself to Higher Cognizance
In *Practicing the Power of Now*, profound educator and creator, Eckhart Tolle, praises the estimation of mindfulness by going about as an observer to your contemplations. To cite, "So when you tune in to an idea, you know of the idea as well as of yourself as the observer of the idea. Another element of awareness has come in."

Have you had a go at being an observer of your considerations? It's life-changing.

The excellence of figuring out how to be mindful at any age is that it permits you to communicate your contemplations at your degree of truth and genuineness while empowering you to burrow for more profound comprehension.

 Try not to stop there. Truly, continue onward. There is in every case more comprehensive insight to find.

"Let us respect each other where we stand, knowing we each move through an amazing trip toward higher awareness."

6. Be Greater Than Your Body
Ask any Zen Master or Yogi and she or he will reveal to you that your character isn't enveloped with your considerations. However, it's one of the reasons for the human existential emergency.

As you climb Abraham Maslow's Hierarchy of Needs toward self-actualization, you will come to understand that you are considerably more than your body. Just in the total combination of psyche, body, and soul would you be able to see past fundamental survivalist attitude with the goal that you start to flourish!

7. Realize You Are Sufficient
Brain, body, and soul acknowledgment is satisfaction all by itself!

There is no more prominent legitimacy than to know who you truly are as part of the unending. More prominent is the endowment of YOU.

As a controlling light, you currently offer others, by model, a similar opportunity. Not, at this point confounded, doing great normally follows as you move from a position of selfishness to one of administration to humankind.

Are your decisions today loaded up with adoration?

Your Valid Life
As part of a development, supported by the apparatuses of innovation, human awareness is extending quicker than any time in recent memory. Living multidimensional as a main priority, body and soul will be your splendid future.

Exemplifying cognizance, your new, credible life will make a huge difference for you. Your magic is currently working for you, rather than the other way around.

You will wake up empowered in the first part of the day, eager to be alive because you're truly communicating. You will feel engaged as things you hate vanish. Opportunity and flourishing will stream plentifully in your life.

The significance of mindfulness is totally obvious to you. You will see the world and the universe supporting you consistently.

It got you here, isn't that right?

EMMA CAMPBELL

SECTION 3—PRACTICAL APPROACHES

CHAPTER 14

HOW TO HANDLE YOUR MISTAKES

We commit errors every now and again. Some regular mistakes we may make include: making a blunder on a solid assignment (composing, diagramming, and so on), irritating somebody, accomplishing something you lament, and participating in unsafe circumstances. Since mishaps are normal, it is imperative to figure out how to fix and adapt to them. Tackling any botch includes: understanding your mistake, making an arrangement, taking part in self-care, and conveying fittingly.

Understanding Your Mistake

1. Distinguish your mistake.
You should initially comprehend what you fouled up to transform it.

Characterize the mistake. Did you say something incorrectly? Did you inadvertently commit an error on a task at work or school? Did you neglect to clean the washroom as you guaranteed?

See how and why you committed the error. Did you do it intentionally and think twice about it? Is it accurate to say that you were not giving it enough consideration? Ponder something like, "How could I neglect to clean the restroom? Did I not have any desire to clean it and stay away from it? Did I get excessively occupied?"

If you don't know what you fouled up, ask somebody (companion, relative, instructor, colleague, chief) to assist you with discovering.

For instance, if somebody is angry with you, you can ask, "I sense that you are annoyed with me, would you be able to clarify this?" This individual may then say, "I'm annoyed with you since you said you would clean the washroom and you didn't do it."

2. Recollect your past mistakes.
Look at your examples of conduct and how you have had comparative issues before. Are there different occasions when you neglected to accomplish something?

Record any examples or subjects you notice that keep coming up for you. This may assist you with distinguishing a bigger objective that you have to chip away at. (ability to focus, certain aptitudes, and so on.) For instance, maybe you will overlook undertakings that you would prefer not to do like cleaning. This could demonstrate you are maintaining a strategic distance from the assignment or that you have to turn out to be progressively sorted out to make sure to finish certain duties.

3. Assume liability.
Comprehend that your mistake is your own. Assume the liability is yours and abstain from accusing somebody else. If you refuse to accept responsibility for the issues at hand, then you can't gain from your flaws, and you may keep committing similar errors again and again.

Record the parts of the issue that you added to or the particular mistake you made.

Distinguish things you may have done another way to create a superior result.

Making an Arrangement

1. Consider past arrangements.
One of the most ideal approaches is to tackle an issue or mistake to recognize how you have tackled comparable issues or mistakes before. Think about considerations like, "I have recollected things before, how could I do that? Goodness no doubt, I kept in touch with them in my schedule and checked it a few times each day!"

Commit a rundown of comparable errors you've made. Recognize how you managed each mistake and if it profited you or not. If it didn't, at that point it presumably won't work.

2. Consider your options.
Think of the same number of potential approaches to fix the mistake. In the present model, there are numerous choices: you could clean the restroom, apologize, offer to clean another part of the house, arrange, plan to do it the next day, and so on.

Utilize your critical thinking abilities to consider potential answers for your present issue.

Make an advantages and disadvantages list for every conceivable arrangement. For instance, if you distinguished that one potential answer for your issue of neglecting to clean the restroom is to make a point to clean it tomorrow, the advantages and disadvantages rundown may resemble this: Pros—the washroom will get spotless in the long run. Cons—it won't be perfect today, I may overlook it tomorrow (I can't guarantee that it will complete), it doesn't assist with taking care of my concern of neglecting to clean the washroom. In light of this appraisal, it might be smarter to clean the washroom that day or build up a memorable arrangement to clean it later on.

3. Settle on a game-plan and do it.
To fix a difficult situation, you should have an arrangement. Recognize the most ideal arrangement and accessible choices, then focus on completing the task.

Finish. If you cause a guarantee to fix the issue, then do it. Being reliable is significant in building trust with others and framing enduring connections.

4. Figure out a back-up plan.
Regardless of how fool-proof the arrangement is, there is a chance it won't fix the issue. For instance, you may clean the restroom, yet the person who requested that you clean it could be angry with you.

Distinguish other potential arrangements and record them from the most generally supportive to the least accommodating. Go down the rundown through and through. The rundown may incorporate things like: offer to tidy up another room, apologize abundantly, ask the individual how he needs you to compensate for it or offer the individual something he appreciates. (nourishment, activities, and so on.)

5. Forestall future mistakes.
If you can effectively discover an answer for your blunder, at that point you are starting the procedure of accomplishment later on and evading mistakes.

Record what you figure you fouled up. At that point record an objective of what you need to do later on. For instance, if you neglected to clean the restroom, you could distinguish objectives like recording a rundown of undertakings every day, check the rundown two times every day, mark off the assignments once they are done, and put update post-its on the ice chest for top need errands.

Practicing Self-Care

1. Offer yourself a reprieve.
Comprehend that it is alright to commit errors. You may feel remorseful, however, it is essential to acknowledge yourself despite your weaknesses.

Pardon yourself and proceed onward as opposed to dwelling on your issue.

Concentrate on improving now and later on.

2. Hold your emotions under wraps.
At the point when we commit an error, it is anything but difficult to get disappointed, overpowered, or surrender. If you are feeling excessively emotional or stressed, enjoy a reprieve. It won't be an advantage to attempt to fix your mistake if your emotions are increased.

3. Adapt.
Concentrate on methods for adapting to negative emotions that may cause you to feel better. Consider ways you have adapted to committing errors in the past. Distinguish ways you have adapted well and ways you adapted that aggravated how you feel. Some regular adapting procedures for managing mistakes include: positive self-talk (expressing pleasant things about yourself), work out, and loosening up activities like playing a game.

Some unhelpful methods for adapting to mistakes drawing in from self-dangerous practices like utilizing liquor or different substances, hurting yourself, ruminating, and the contemplation of the self.

Esteem

1. Be assertive.

Utilizing assertive relational abilities implies saying how you think and feel in a deferential and proper way. When you are assertive, you concede when you are incorrect and take responsibility for individual deficiencies. You don't reprimand others for your mistakes.

Maintain a strategic distance from detachment, which includes abstaining from discussing it, covering up, obliging what everybody needs you to do, and not defending yourself.

Try not to be aggressive, including raising your voice, hollering, deprecating, reviling, and brutal practices. (tossing things, hitting.)

Abstain from being passive-aggressive. This is a blend among passive and aggressive types of correspondence where you might be disturbed, however, not be inevitable with your emotions. Along these lines, you may accomplish something despite somebody's good faith to seek retribution or give them the silent treatment. This isn't the best type of correspondence and the individual may not comprehend what you are attempting to convey or why.

Send positive nonverbal messages. Our nonverbal communication sends messages to the individuals around us. The first and most obvious, sign to nonverbal communication is a person's facial expressions. Even though we only have one face, it can show a wealth of expressions. From a half-smile to a full-blown smirk, to a casual eye shift, our facial expressions reveal a range of emotions. Instead of delving into all the nuances like a quirk of the lip or a twitch of the eye, let's take a look at the three most prominent expressions:

- Smiling - A smile generally indicates happiness or contentment.

- Scowling - A scowl or frown indicates discontentment or frustration.

- Lack of Expression - An expressionless face can indicate, at a minimum, two things. First, this can be an indication of disinterest or boredom. Second, and perhaps worse, an expressionless face can indicate disdain.

An expressionless face is hard to decipher, so if you suspect you're exhibiting what's known as a "stone" face, it might be nice to pop in a gentle smile from time to time.

2. Use active listening abilities.
Let the person vent his disappointments and hold up to respond.

Attempt to concentrate exclusively on tuning in to the person as opposed to pondering how to react. Concentrate on the other individual's sentiments and considerations rather than your own.

Offer rundown expressions and pose explaining inquiries like, "I hear you saying that you are irate because I neglected to clean the washroom, is that right?"

Identify. Attempt to be understanding and put yourself in the other person's shoes.

3. Apologize.
At the point when we commit errors, we at times hurt others. Saying you are sorry shows that you lament the mistake, feel terrible about the damage you've done, and that you need to improve in the future.

Try not to part with reasons or attempt to clarify it. Just own ready. State, "I concede I neglected to clean the washroom. I am so grieved about that."

Be mindful so as not to accuse others. Try not to state something like, "If you would have reminded me to clean it, at that point perhaps I would have recalled and done it."

4. Commit to positive change.
Communicating approaches to compensate for the issue and focusing on dealing with the issues are powerful approaches to fix a mistake when it includes someone else.

Attempt to work out an answer. Ask the individual what they might want you to do to compensate for it. You could state, "Is there anything that I can do now?"

Make sense of how to do things another way later on. You can ask the person, "What might help me not commit this error once more?"

Tell the individual that you are happy to place in the work to lessen the probability of committing the error later on. You could state something like, "I don't need this to happen again so I will put forth an attempt to _____." Say exactly what you will do, for example, "I will ensure I record a rundown of my errands with the goal that I won't overlook once more."

CHAPTER 15
HOW TO ACCEPT PAST MISTAKES

Mistakes are part of being human. Everybody commits errors every now and again. If you need to relinquish your past, change your mindset. Remember you can take in an exercise from your mistakes and quit seeing them as inalienably awful. If you want to offer some kind of reparation for a past mistake, find a way to do as such. In conclusion, acknowledge yourself. Self-acknowledgment is critical for proceeding onward.

Changing Your Mindset

1. Perceive the basic emotions beneath your second thoughts.
In case you're experiencing difficulty getting over a mistake, there might be an explanation you can't give up. Invest some energy attempting to recognize fundamental emotions underneath deplorable conduct. To relinquish the past, you should have the option to discharge certain emotions that binds you to a mistake.

Would it be that your partner made this mistake? Do you sense that you passed something up? Do you have an inclination that you fouled up by a friend or family member? Would you be able to recognize a solitary emotion, or a few emotions, that bind you to your past?

For instance, perhaps you feel it was a mistake to turn down an opening for work. You feel saddened over what could have been. Attempt to manage sentiments of disappointment head-on. Work on tolerating that everybody has lamented and that they're a typical part of life. This will assist you with relinquishing an apparent mistake.

2. Separate yourself from your mistakes.
Frequently, we can't proceed onward because we consider mistakes to be poor conduct as characterizing our character. Everybody commits errors and takes part in poor conduct. Such conduct doesn't mirror your qualities and worth as an individual. Figure out how to consider yourself to be a different substance from the mistakes you've made.

Attempt to regard yourself as you would treat someone else. If a friend or family member committed a similar error you did, what might you say? Odds are, you would not think a companion or relative is an awful individual in light of a solitary lack of foresight.

Award yourself this equivalent generosity. Because you botched up doesn't mean you're a terrible individual. You and your mistakes are two unique things. You can utilize mistakes to recognize approaches to change yourself, yet your terrible characteristics don't speak to all that you are as an individual.

3. Search for an exercise.
You might be better ready to acknowledge your mistakes if you feel they were advantageous. Rather than ruminating over what you could have improved, stop and think about what you can realize. You can't change the past, yet you can utilize it to control yourself towards better decisions in the future.

Attempt to encourage an appreciation to gain some new useful knowledge. For instance, if you discover that you get baffled when your mother attempts to converse with you with showing up at home, at that point, it can be appreciative of discovering that you need some opportunity to decompress after you return home. This is something new that you have found out about yourself that can assist you in developing better associations with the individuals who are near you.

Blame is your brain's method for sending you an admonition sign that you have to change. In case you're feeling remorseful, your conduct might be excessively extraordinary or undesirable in one way or another. In case you're fixating on a past mistake, stop and consider what you can realize.

For instance, perhaps you were having a stressful day at work and took it out on your mother. You may have to figure out how to control your emotions more as opposed to lashing out at others. You can't change how you acted previously, however, going ahead can allow you to attempt control over your emotions.

4. Acknowledge you're defective.
You should have the option to relinquish a requirement for flawlessness. If you can't get over past mistakes, you may have inclinations. Recollect that nobody is great, and you can't anticipate that you should experience life without ever making mistakes.

Advise yourself that you're ready to perceive your mistakes. Numerous individuals can't perceive when they've made a mistake and will proceed down a terrible way. The fact you're self-mindful will work well for you.

Not committing errors isn't reasonable. You have to acknowledge that you've made blunders and are blemished here and there. For whatever length of time that you're ready to perceive your mistakes, you're on the right path.

5. Recognize that you acted with a restricted mindfulness.
As life goes on, we are continually learning and developing. Your qualities and convictions may even change. Something that seems clear to you now may not have been evident a couple of years back because you didn't have similar information or convictions that you have now.

For instance, you may have had a go at utilizing a medication like cocaine quite a long while prior because you figured it may be entertaining. Presently, you may realize this is a profoundly addictive medication that may lead you to act in manners that are not consistent with what your identity is. In any case, at the time that you attempted it, you didn't have this information.

Or, on the other hand, you may have confided in somebody who deceived you and think back on this. In any case, you had no chance of realizing that this individual may sell you out.

Presenting Appropriate Reparations in Light of Your Mistakes

1. Perceive blame is helpful.
The initial step to presenting appropriate reparations is grasping your blame. Rather than attempting to overlook or excuse it, see what you can realize. In case you're feeling remorseful, this is because you've accomplished something incorrectly. You may need to compensate for this, and change your conduct in the future.

Consider why you're feeling regretful. Did you hurt somebody you care about? Did you lash out at a companion or relative? What would you be able to improve later on? What would be a good idea for you to do to compensate for it in the present?

Be that as it may, don't pass into disgrace. Disgrace is the point where you judge your entire self-dependent on a couple of actions. This is counterproductive and will lead you to feel awful about yourself without rolling out any profitable improvements. As you recognize your blame, recall terrible actions and decisions that don't make you an awful individual.

2. Accept what you fouled up.
It's essential to have the option to confess to mistakes without rationalizing, particularly if you've harmed someone else. To change and offer some kind of reparation, you have to perceive your conduct was a problem.

Abstain from rationalizing yourself. Try not to think, "Indeed, I spoke harshly to my companions, however, I had a great deal of stress going on", or "Truly, I was troublesome yesterday, yet my youth makes me act along these lines."

In case you're rationalizing, you're bound to let awful conduct slide later on. Rather, contemplate internally, "I committed an error. I can't change that, however, I can take a shot at improving it later on."

3. Foster empathy.
 If you need to compensate for your mistakes, attempt to know how you hurt somebody. Consider what you said or did. Envision how the other individual felt being forced to bear your behavior.

It may not be anything but difficult to have empathy. This might be particularly evident in case you're taking a shot at proceeding onward. In case you're excusing yourself, you may ponder the other person you hurt. Self-pardoning can be troublesome.

To truly resolve to transform, you have to remain compassionate. Invest a great deal of energy thinking about how you hurt somebody, and imagining that person's perspective. This will assist you with easing back down and consider your actions more later on.

4. Figure out how to make it right.
This might be as basic as a conciliatory sentiment. You may also need to locate a solid method to compensate for your actions. In the wake of thinking about your mistake and tolerating fault, attempt to make up for it with the other person.

Now and again, it might be clear on what to do. If you, for instance, harmed somebody's property, you have to fix it. If you obtained cash and didn't return it, you have to bring it back.

In different cases, the harm is less concrete. You may need to apologize to somebody and attempt to tell them you've changed. It might require some investment to reconstruct a harmed relationship, yet it will merit the exertion. This will assist you with tolerating your mistakes and push ahead.

In different cases, the issue might be close to home. While you didn't hurt any other individual, you let yourself down. If you settled on a poor decision, consider how you can improve it later on. You can also see approaches to fix the harm now. For instance, say you overspent this month because of going out with companions and superfluous costs. You could be exacting with spending until your next check.

Tolerating Yourself

1. See yourself in less high contrast terms.
If you experience difficulty relinquishing mistakes, this might be identified with your perspective. You may tend to see things, including yourself, in highly contrasting terms. If you will view life as an issue of right versus off-base and great versus terrible, attempt to chip away at seeing the dim area.

Quit assessing yourself. You don't have to put a name on your conduct. It's alright to concede you need to change, or that you loathed your actions in a given circumstance, however, it might be counterproductive to mark certain practices as dispassionately off-base.

Attempt to acknowledge yourself. A few actions are uncertain and befuddling. You can commit an error without expecting to arrange your actions, or yourself, by an exacting division.

2. Give yourself grace.
Do you give yourself a similar grace you show others? If not, it might be an opportunity to do as such. In case you're not being thoughtful to yourself, it will be more enthusiastically for you to relinquish your past and move forward.

Attempt to acknowledge what your identity is, regardless of mistakes. If you have dear companions or relatives, odds are you're mindful of their defects. Does that mean you couldn't care less about them? No. Attempt to give yourself this equivalent graciousness.

Stop issue musings as they happen. If you begin to believe, "I'm so distraught at myself for messing up. I'm such a disappointment", supplant these ideas with positive contemplations. You could, for instance, think something like, "I committed an error, yet it's alright I have defects. I'm content with myself."

3. Grasp your qualities.

It's critical to recognize your qualities close by your mistakes. If you wind up ruminating over past mistakes, stop and help yourself to remember all that you do right.

Take a stab at recording your qualities when you're feeling negative about yourself. Take a pen and paper and scribble down what you like about yourself.

You can begin with something essential like, "I'm nice to other people." Build on that and list qualities that are explicit to you.

CHAPTER 16
HOW TO DEAL WITH CRITICISM

Criticism is terrible, regardless of whether it's originating from a well-importance English educator or your curve reticent foe. If the criticism is intended to be productive, at that point you can utilize it to turn into a well-adjusted person. What's more, if it's just intended to hurt you, you can chip away at shaking it off like a negative behavior pattern. So how would you manage it? Peruse this means to discover.

Changing Your Perspective

1. Know the contrast between damaging and useful criticism.
This is the initial step to being ready to manage criticism. You need to know where the feedback is coming from and comprehend the expectations of the individual who is offering it to you. If it's from an instructor, at that point chances are the person needs you to perform better; yet when it's originating from an alleged companion, a toxic acquaintance, or even an adversary, at that point you need to ponder whether the person has your well-being as a primary concern.

In case you're certain that the criticism is invalid and intended to hurt you, at that point, you can avoid them to figure out how to manage dangerous criticism.

Useful criticism is, in a perfect world, intended to support you. Ruinous criticism is just planned to cause harm.

Attempt to concentrate on the message. It's difficult to see that an individual is truly disclosing to you something genuine that you can take a shot at if the person is shouting at you or simply acting like you're a nuisance.

2. Acknowledge that you're not great.
This is an extraordinary method to manage criticism. If you need to have the option to take a little bit of feedback, at that point you can't continue imagining that you can't take the blame no matter what. No one's ideal, so if you believe you're great, at that point you're no one. Yet genuinely: every individual has defects, and if you don't perceive any of yours, at that point you're not dissecting yourself as you should.

Make a rundown of your ten greatest defects. Believe it or not. Ten! Would you be able to consider ten things that need improvement? What about fifteen? This activity isn't intended to cause you to feel awful about yourself; it's just intended to make you see that you have the opportunity to get better.

Consider the people you know. Would you be able to name a solitary one who is impeccable and who isn't a famous actor? Also, recollect that even most famous actors have a few defects, even though it could be noticeably little.

3. Try not to think about it.
If you need to realize the best arrangement with criticism, at that point you can't think about it literally. If your manager says you've been somewhat less beneficial than expected, it's not because he believes you're fat and sluggish; this is because he needs you, his worker, to step up your game. If your closest companion says that

you tend to daydream when she's conversing with you, don't feel that she's calling you a loathsome companion and a zombie; she simply needs you to communicate a little better.

If the criticism is valuable, at that point it's proposed to direct and enable you to improve as a person, not to cut you down and cause you to feel lacking.

If your educator has given you rather basic feedback on a paper, it's not because she believes you're inept or irritating in class; this is because she thinks you have some work to do to make a contention.

4. Work on being less delicate.
If you generally wind up crying, getting guarded, and feeling commonly agitated when somebody gives you what should be useful feedback, at that point you need to begin thickening your skin. Work on tolerating your defects and being ready to catch wind of certain zones where you can improve. If you never improve, at that point, you'll be level coating, and you don't need that. Attempt to concentrate on the message and its expectation to help you as opposed to concentrating on the entirety of the 'significant' or 'frightful' things that were said to you.

Consider where the message is coming from. Odds are, your supervisor didn't simply send you a short email to cause you to feel terrible. He most likely needs you to carry out your responsibility better. Check your emotions. You don't have to tear up every time someone says a negative word.

Work on your notoriety. If people think you are touchy, they will be less inclined to come clean with you, and you don't need people to feel like they're strolling around on eggshells whenever they converse with you.

Managing Constructive Criticism

1. Comprehend what you're truly being told.
If you need to manage criticism, at that point you need to comprehend the message behind it. If you've verified that the criticism is intended to be productive, you need to separate it so you can begin making sense of what to do straight away. Here and there, you might be centered around the harmful parts of the feedback and your pride might be injured for you to perceive what is directly before you.

Of course, you weren't content with the 'C' on your English paper. In any case, was your educator attempting to reveal to you that you were dumb and an unpleasant essayist? Likely not. She needed to advise you to look into your content more, and to go through with solid proof to back your cases. It also wouldn't have harmed to meet them as far as possible, would it?

If your companion revealed to you you're fixated on yourself, that would surely harm you. Could there be something useful behind the message? Your companion is instructing you to be somewhat more compassionate and to invest more energy pondering others and less time contemplating yourself. Listen and take the time to improve without having to take things too personally.

2. Check whether there's some fact to it.
If the feedback is originating from an individual who has your well-being as a primary concern, at that point you need to think about how conceivable it is that there is some reality to those words. It's significantly more probable that you've heard comparable remarks before.

If ten individuals revealed how you were selfish, or if your last three lady friends disclosed you were emotionally distant, then at that point they can't all be right, can they? Pause for a minute to think about how conceivable it is that this person is truly on to something.

3. Make a game arrangement for tending to it.
Okay, you've concluded that your English instructor, chief, beau, or closest companion is right. You must record the thing you have to deal with, and arrange to tend to it. This can take quite a while, and it's never past the point where it is possible to begin. When you think of an arrangement—a method for modifying your desires and actions—you can start to address the criticism and become a superior individual.

If your English instructor is expecting you to accomplish more research, try investing twice as much energy finding out about your sources before you think of a contention next time.

If your supervisor reveals you're disrupted, take a shot at arranging your work area, Inbox, and your spreadsheets until you feel more in charge.

If your beau reveals you're excessively destitute, take a shot at giving him some space by investing more energy alone or with your lady friends.

4. Thank the individual for being straightforward (if he's being caring)
If you have gotten some criticism that was conveyed in an inviting and accommodating manner or just in a way that was intended to be straightforward and clear, at that point set aside the effort to thank the person and state that you value how they revealed to you something that can make you a far superior companion or sweetheart.

Expressing gratitude toward individuals who give you genuine criticism is also an indication of development. Suck it up and state 'thank you' regardless of if you're gritting your teeth or not.

5. Quit rationalizing.
If somebody is giving you legitimate criticism, quit rationalizing why that person is off-base, particularly if you realize that there is some fact to what the individual is stating. If you get guarded and rationalize, at that point the person won't have the option to complete the process of letting you know exactly what they mean, and you won't get the information you need to truly improve. It's normal that we feel cautious and get the inclination that we can't be blamed under any circumstance, however, it's critical to listen to people before you slice them off to demonstrate you're perfect.

If somebody is sincerely busy disclosing something to you that you can do to improve yourself, don't state, "However, I as of now do that..." except if you feel like the person is truly misguided.

If your instructor says you have to work more earnestly, don't give her a faltering reason for why you've been relaxing. Rather, note the feedback and attempt to address it.

It takes development to remain calm as opposed to rationalizing why the person isn't right when you're getting substantial feedback.

6. Recall that useful criticism can make you a superior individual.
Without a doubt, it's hard to manage even the most well-importance criticism, particularly if you're persuaded, you're great and you can't be blamed for any circumstance. Yet, if you've put in resources into being a magnificent person, at that point help yourself by being mindful to remember your imperfections and weaknesses. Making an

arrangement for tending to them will make you into a more astonishing person.

Whenever you hear some valuable criticism, grasp it! It's sort of like what Kelly Clarkson stated: "Whatever (criticism in our case) doesn't kill you, makes you stronger. Stand a little taller."

Managing Destructive Criticism

After you have concluded that the valuable criticism is justified, the primary thing you ought to do is what follows.

1. Comprehend the person's actual intentions.
If you have perceived the criticism as totally damaging and frightful, at that point you can consider why the individual may have said something like this to cause yourself to feel better. Possibly the young lady was jealous of your new outfit and said you dress like a whore. Maybe a person said you're not a decent essayist since he's jealous that you distributed a story. Perhaps the individual was simply feeling terrible and wanted to take it out on somebody. Whatever the explanation, advise yourself that it had little to do with what your identity is.

Come to the situation from the person's perspective. Comprehend what he is truly used to. Neglecting the fact that the words will even now sting, it may cause you to feel better. If it happens that your collaborator shouted at you for reasons unknown, yet you recollect that he is experiencing a separation, at that point you'll begin to understand more, won't you?

2. Search for the trace of legitimacy.
Okay, so perhaps the criticism was conveyed in a manner that was mean, superfluous, and frightful, and the greater part of the things

that were said were off base. Perhaps your associate said you were "a finished chaos" or your companion said you were "absolutely selfish" for what you believe had no explanation. Pause for a moment to consider it, however: do you have to catch up on your authoritative abilities? Have you been known to be somewhat selfish every once in a while? Provided that this is true, at that point you ought to reevaluate your actions without getting injured by how the criticism was given to you.

Without a doubt, it's difficult to pay attention to somebody in a situation where they are hollering at you or calling you names. This makes it almost difficult to pay attention to a word they state. Be that as it may if you need to be the greater individual, attempt to locate the basic message if there is one.

3. Recollect that words can never hurt you.
What was that thing your mom informed you regarding 'sticks and stones' not being ready to break your bones? Without a doubt, you thought it was dumb in third grade, yet now, you're significantly more seasoned, and it's beginning to bode well. At long last, dangerous criticism isn't comprised of slugs, blades, or nuclear bombs. It's only a progression of words associated together in a manner intended to cause you to feel horrendous. Along these lines, advise yourself that criticism comprises of a lot of words. Criticism can't take your cash, smack you over the face, or crash your vehicle. So don't let it get to you.

4. Remain certain.
The most significant thing you can do is keep up your confidence. Regardless of what individuals are stating about you, you need to

remain solid. Recall what your identity is and don't let others impact your self-worth. Being certain doesn't mean reasoning that you're impeccable, however, it means adoring what your identity is and what you look like. If you're genuinely certain, at that point you won't let haters get you down and make you consider less of yourself.

In case you're discontent with what your identity is, wonder why. Make a rundown of a couple of things you don't care for about yourself and make sense of what you can change.

Being certain also implies tolerating the things you can't change about yourself. In this way, you don't care that you're so tall. Do you plan on slumping, or will you begin to cherish your long legs?

Spending time with people who cause you to feel great about yourself will also go far in causing you to feel increasingly sure. In a scenario you're hanging out with people who continually cut you down. At that point you better believe it, you're not going to like yourself.

5. Continue doing what you're doing.
So...you've heard that somebody said you're a toad. Will you begin participating less in class? Or, on the other hand, your colleague has disclosed to you you're also type A. Is it accurate to say that you are going to quit being what your identity is if it's working for you? Absolutely not. If you haven't got a legitimate criticism and realize that individuals are letting you know is just being said due to desire, anger, or dastardliness, at that point there's no compelling reason to change your everyday practice to please individuals.

If the criticism has no premise at all, at that point the best thing you can do is to disregard it.

Try not to feel terrible in case you're not ready to push with or without these negative words immediately. It takes practice to quit thinking about what individuals think.

SELF CONFIDENCE AND SELF-ESTEEM

CHAPTER 17

HOW TO OVERCOME LOW SELF ESTEEM

If you find out that you have low self-esteem, it influences each part of your life and detracts from your pleasure and bliss. Beating low self-esteem can be cultivated if someone is eager to work at it. It doesn't occur incidentally, and it takes a great deal of work and persistence, however, the result is well worth the exertion.

Improving Your Self-Esteem

1. Perceive that numerous people experience the ill effects of low self-esteem.
You are not the only one. In an ongoing report, research found that 4% of single ladies around the globe see themselves as beautiful.

2. Recognize the musings, sentiments, physical indications, and practices related to low self-esteem.
Numerous individuals mistake these musings, practices, and sentiments with characteristics. In any case, negative considerations are not equivalent to actual characteristics. These kinds of contemplations, sentiments, physical signs, and practices resemble 'indications' of low self-esteem.

Perceiving the side effects will enable you to recognize what musings, emotions, and practices should be focused on for development.

3. Tune in to your inward monologue.

At the point when a large number of the accompanying musings happen, it resembles you're hearing a voice inside your head. These considerations are frequently programmed, practically like a reflex.

- I'm excessively feeble/not gifted enough/not savvy enough.

- I trust they don't believe I'm an American.

- I'm excessively fat/meager/old/youthful/and so on.

- Everything is my shortcoming.

- I think I must be impeccable when I perform at my specific employment.

- My supervisor doesn't care for my report. I should be a complete disappointment at my specific employment.

- Why have a go at meeting new individuals? They won't care for me.

4. Pinpoint how it is you feel about yourself.
Emotions, similar to musings, regularly originate from an internal discourse that doesn't precisely mirror the facts.

- I feel so embarrassed that my manager didn't care for my report.

- I'm so irate at myself that my manager didn't care for my report.

- I'm so baffled at my manager censuring me.

- I feel restless/frozen when I'm with people who I don't know since they're most likely pondering how fat I am.

- I'm not sufficiently able to contend, so I won't attempt.

- I feel on edge more often than not.

5. Search for physical signs that identify with low self-esteem.
The next might be physical signs that you have low self-esteem.

- I can't rest more often than not.

- I am worn out more often than not.

- My body feels tense.

At the point when I meet a new individual (or I'm in another awkward circumstance):

- I sweat lavishly.

- The room turns.

- I can't regain some composure.

- I redden a great deal.

- I feel like my heart is going to explode from out of my chest.

6. Survey your conduct to check whether your self-esteem is impacting your life.
If you find that at least one of these conduct proclamations concern you, your self-esteem might be greatly affecting the way you live.

- I don't go out/I don't care for individuals to see me, or me them.

- I experience difficulty in deciding.

- I don't feel good communicating my suppositions or supporting myself.

- I don't believe I'm fit for taking care of a new position, regardless of whether it is an advancement.

- I get agitated without any problem.

- I contend with the individuals throughout my life a lot.

- I get protective and shout at my family.

- My companion calls me 'Feline' constantly and I don't care for it, yet I'm apprehensive of the fact that if I say anything, she won't be my companion.

- I'm too self-cognizant to engage in sexual relations.

- I engage in sexual relations in any event when I would prefer not to.

- All that I do must be great.

- I eat well past being full.

- I can't eat more than one supper daily or I'll get excessively fat.

7. Distinguish your negative musings.

Regardless of whether you understand it or not, your considerations in your mind are catching you inside the pattern of low self-esteem. To feel improved, it's good to recognize when these kinds of considerations are going on, and discover approaches to conquer them. There are some common negative self-articulations you can get comfortable with, so if you run over some of them, you can target them for elimination.

8. Try not to be a nagger, putter-killjoy, or a name-guest.
Envision you have a 'companion' who is continually close by, and this companion continually upbraids you. The person calls you awful names, reveals to you that you are doing everything incorrectly, you're good for nothing, you'll accomplish nothing, and you're unlikable. Wouldn't that get you down?

9. Abstain from being a generalist.
The generalist will make a mistake, an event where the person in question didn't perform to desires or exceed expectations.

For instance, if an individual strides into a pothole, she may have these contemplations that she was summing up: "For what reason do things like this consistently transpire? I'm simply reviled. I never have any good karma whatsoever."

10. Battle the inclination to be a comparer.
People who contrast consistently feel insufficient because individuals of this kind of thought design are constantly contrasting themselves and others, and accepting that everybody around them is superior to them.

For example, a comparer may state this: "Take a look at that. My neighbor has a Hemi truck. I don't know if I would ever bear the cost of one of those. I'm such a disappointment."

11. Evade the voice that transforms you into a person that catastrophizes.
People who catastrophize make conclusions about their whole lives and depend on one episode.

This is what a catastrophizer may think: "I got a B in this class rather than an A. I'll never get a new line of work."

12. Recall that you are not a mind reader.
Psyche readers consistently believe that people think the most noticeably awful thing about them. In actuality, we don't generally have the foggiest idea of what others are thinking.

Mind readers tend to make suspicions about what others are thinking or the reasons they are getting things done, and the brain reader considerations are constantly slanted: "That person is gazing at me. He's most likely reasoning what a monstrosity I am."

13. Focus on wiping out negative musings.
With this negative information, it's no big surprise self-esteem endures. If you perceive your ineffective idea designs, you can battle them. It requires some investment and tolerance because changing old propensities takes a great deal of work. Making it in little strides is exceptionally useful.

It's simpler to do small amounts of progress, and it's simpler to start treating yourself well by intuition in a positive manner.

14. Separate among supposition and fact.
Ordinarily, it tends to be hard to perceive what is a feeling and what is a fact. Our inward considerations are frequently conclusions, regardless of whether we think they are facts.

A fact is an unquestionable explanation, for example, "I am twenty-two years of age." You have the birth declaration to demonstrate it.

Assessments are not unquestionable. A case of an assessment is: "I'm constantly inept."

This announcement is refutable. Some may believe it's not, and they will offer proof of times where they believe they were idiotic, for example, "I'm so inept, I tumbled off the phase when I was eight." However, while investigating this experience, a person can get familiar with a couple of things, for example, an adult was answerable for supervising the task, so that person ought to have thought about your well-being.

People are not great and commit errors. Indeed, even Einstein has conceded a few mistakes in his career. This shows nobody is extremely dumb if they commit errors. Indeed, even virtuoso's commit errors.

Regardless of whether you have encounters supporting your negative convictions, you ought to also have encounters supporting when you've settled on incredible decisions and have done some extremely shrewd things.

Utilizing a Journal to Improve Self-Esteem

1. Start a self-esteem journal.
Since you know a few reasons why the loss of self-esteem happens and the fundamental negative considerations that are answerable for sustaining low self-esteem, you can start the procedure to change your convictions about yourself. This procedure may be simpler to do on the PC, so you can change the association around so it sounds good to you without beginning your journal once more. A spreadsheet position is a decent method to keep your musings organized and permits you a lot of space to experiment.

2. Become a negative idea investigator.

For a couple of days, monitor your negative musings. You can keep these in a paper scratchpad, on a calendar function on a PC or your iPad. Watch all the negative articulations you make to yourself. In a situation where you don't remember them by type, it's alright. Record the announcement at any rate.

For instance, one of the things on the rundown was, "I'm going to come up short if I want to or even attempt to make it as an essayist," with related contemplations: "Why is this even trouble? Nobody will like it in any case. Nobody has anything unique to state in any case. It's been composed before."

3. Arrange your list.
Title this section: 'Negative Thoughts'. Put the contemplations into request, the highest point of the page containing the ones that trouble you the most, and the base musings that make you the least resentful. If you see various kinds of articulations that share something for all intents and purpose, bunch them together.

For instance, "I will fall flat if I attempt to make it as an author" is at the highest priority on the list. All related negative considerations can be incorporated with this idea, yet the lead sentence can be thought of as the title for this estimation.

4. Discover the foundation of each negative idea.
Make a section close to your 'Negative Thoughts' segment and call it 'Memory/Experience Associated With This Thought'. A person or experience may ring a bell. Record it. If not, simply leave it clear. Understanding where you've been will assist you with acknowledging why you feel the way you do.

For instance, "My dad disclosed to me I would come up short if I end up attempting to be an author."

Keep in mind, if you recall that somebody expressed a negative remark to you, this isn't a fact! It's just their assessment, and you will have the option to figure out how to disprove it.

Note: If this progression makes you so annoyed that it's hard for you to work on for the remainder of the day or week, or makes it hard for you to proceed, stop and look for proficient treatment.

5. Distinguish emotions related to each idea.
In the following section, titled 'The Way This Thought Makes Me Feel', record any emotions you may have related to this negative proclamation. This will assist you with the understanding that your contemplations influence your emotions.

For instance, "It makes me want to surrender."

6. Distinguish your practices.
The following section state, 'How I Act When I Think and Feel Like This'. Then attempt to think about an ongoing occasion that will assist you in acknowledging how you act. Do you get tranquil? Do you shout? Do you cry? Do you stay away from eye to eye connection with individuals? This will assist you with perceiving how your considerations and emotions are interconnected with the way with which you act.

For instance, "When I saw challenges or solicitations to compose, I disregarded them even though I need to be an author more than anything else."

7. Alter your reasoning.

It's an ideal opportunity to counter your negative suppositions and encounters with positive ones, which will assist you with understanding that the negative explanations are conclusions that hold you down and that you should quit trusting in these negative assessments you have framed yourself with.

8. Counter the pessimism.
Add a section to your journal called 'Rude awakening'. In this segment, put down any characteristic, great memory, achievement, or whatever else that is positive to counteract your negative conviction. If you locate a counter to your conviction, at that point your negative conviction won't hold any fact or legitimacy in your life. The idea you accepted to be a flat-out principle is not the standard.

For instance, "I have had five sonnets distributed, universally! Ha! Take that! I have also had four magazine articles distributed. It's false all things considered. I won't come up short. I've just succeeded!"

9. Make a positive action plan.
In your last section, you can put what you know enthusiastically with 'What I Will Do Now'. For this segment, be liberal with your thoughts on what you will do starting now and into the foreseeable future.

For instance, "I will do all that I can to ensure I succeed. I will return to class for my master's certificate. I will investigate where I can compose and get my articles distributed, and I won't surrender until I get paid work. I will search for composing work. I will participate in challenges. I won't surrender until I win one."

10. Concentrate on your positive traits.
Give a segment of your journal (or another tab in your spreadsheet) to composing positive things about yourself. Rewrite or make a

rundown of your positive characteristics. Anything that will cause you to feel great about yourself and assist you with acknowledging what your identity is, the thing that you've achieved, and how far you've come in your life can be composed on this page. You may decide to concentrate on a few or the entirety of the accompanying:

- Your accomplishments. (for the afternoon, week, month, year.)

- I spared my organization 7,000,000 dollars this year.

- I invested energy with my children consistently.

- I figured out how to deal with my stress so I feel great most days.

- I won an honor.

- I grinned at another person I didn't know today, even though this is hard for me.

- Your properties and qualities.

- I have a bubbly character.

- I can offer an extraordinary compliment.

- I am a great listener.

- I know how to cause the ones I love to feel good.

11. Distinguish areas that you might want to improve.
It is imperative to address ways that you might want to improve without excessively concentrating on thoughts of solidarity or shortcoming. Accepting we are frail or insufficient in one way or another will

be another self-esteem trap. It's awful that this self-vanquishing thought is upheld all through our general public.

Quit considering yourself as far as shortcomings and rather consider territories you might want to improve, and simply because transforming them will fulfill you.

Making objectives for change isn't tied in with fixing something that is broken. It's tied in with doing things that will assist you with working more effectively in your life and assist you with having solid connections, which helps your self-esteem and joy.

In your journal, either make another tab in your spreadsheet—or another page in your paper journal—and consider it the title of this segment: 'Zones I Would Like to Improve'. Then compose underneath it: 'Although it will satisfy me'.

A few instances of progress objectives that are not excessively centered around shortcomings are: I might want to...

- Oversee stress all the more effectively.

- Work on sorting out my desk work.

- Work on getting more organized.

- Make sure to accomplish something I truly appreciate once per day and not feel regretful about it.

- Improve my child-bearing aptitudes.

Changing Your Relationships

1. Surround yourself with positive people.

If you have contrary contemplations in your mind, it's conceivable you have people around you who are expressing similar sorts of negative messages about you, even dear loved ones. As you're improving your self-esteem, if it's conceivable, limit contact with individuals you notice are stating negative comments to you, regardless of whether they are near you or are busy working.

2. Consider negative articulations from others as a ten-pound load.
In a situation where you put on a ten-pound weight for each antagonistic explanation, and you are encircled by people who put you down. In the long run, it turns out to be harder to lift yourself.

Expelling yourself from the weight of tuning in and identifying with antagonistic individuals will cause you to feel lighter since you don't need to hold up under the heaviness of their negative remarks, their negative decisions towards you, or their reluctance to approach you with deference.

Assertiveness urges others to approach you with deference, which will help support positive self-esteem. To put it plainly, assertiveness prevents people's other awful practices from affecting you just as it causes you have sound correspondences with the people around you. You can use a couple of various procedures to practice assertive indifference.

3. Utilize 'I' rather than 'you'.
Instead of saying, "You didn't take out the waste the previous evening," you can state, "I feel upset when guarantees are made and aren't seen through."

The primary proclamation can be taken as an assault and increment the audience's defensiveness. The second is sharing your emotions, and telling the individual what the person in question did to add to those sentiments.

4. Tune in and be eager to settle.
Consider how the people you talk with feel and be eager to reach an accord that satisfies both of you.

For example, if your companion requests that you drive him to the store, you can say, "I can't at present; I have a class. I can drive you a short time later. Would that be alright?"

5. Be tireless without getting aggressive.
You can say no, and you can go for your privileges without hollering, and without surrendering. In case you're experiencing difficulty expressing what is on your mind, *Psychology Tools* suggests utilizing a 'broken record' approach, where you keep up consideration and a wonderful tone.

For instance, if your nearby market sold you an awful bit of meat and won't acknowledge its return, you can say, "I understand. I would like a discount." If after a few endeavors you don't see your outcomes, you can attempt an announcement like this, "If you would prefer not to give me a discount, that is your decision. I can decide to call the Health Department, however, I'd prefer not to. Which would be simpler for the two of us?"

6. Set individual boundaries.
It's your obligation to let your loved ones—as well as associates, friends, and collaborators—how you need to be dealt with. A few practices from others can directly affect your self-esteem if you hear it long enough.

For example, if you conclude you don't need others calling you names, you can tell them you don't care for it and you will make a move or take action if they do not desist from their current path.

If this type of obnoxious attack doesn't stop, make a move, and tell somebody with power that can support you. In case you're grinding away, record a provocation objection. In case you're an understudy, tell your parents, an educator, or your head. Maybe it's a companion, but your companion probably wouldn't have understood that their actions were getting you upset. It's constantly justified despite all the trouble to tell individuals how you feel.

Improving Your Lifestyle

1. Set aside a few minutes for yourself, regardless of whether you are a parent.
Numerous guardians mistakenly remove themselves from the condition when thinking about their children. It's normal to need to concentrate to give them the most ideal condition. Be that as it may, if you quit concentrating and disregard yourself, this can detract you from being the parent you truly need to be.

Guardians are educators to their children. With the goal for instructors to be genuinely powerful, educators must have a type of skill. Also, your very own propensities may come off on them, and this incorporates the awful ones just as the great ones.

Deciding to deal with yourself a couple of moments daily is everything necessary and not exclusively to raise your self-esteem, yet in addition to fill in as an extraordinary model for your children.

If you don't have children, dealing with yourself will assist you with feeling much improved and merits the exertion.

2. Pick healthy nourishments.
Eating healthy nourishment choices may take some underlying arranging from the start that you intend to do a whole way of life makeover. In any case, this can be overwhelming for effectively occupied, stressed-out individuals.

Rather than keeping convoluted arrangements of things you eat or things you ought to eat, settle on a decision to pick a healthy choice at each dinner and bite.

Evade nourishments like confections, pop, cake, doughnuts, and baked goods, which lead to huge vitality crashes, potential cerebral pains, and offer no sustenance, conceivable ailment, and included calories.

3. Eat more natural products, veggies, lean meats, and vegetables.
Consider them throughout the day. Vitality and bottomless sustenance for your body will empower you to stay aware of your activity and children, and ensure your body against sicknesses. This will expand your life so you can appreciate more time with your family.

4. Take a stab at a reasonable eating routine.
A decent meal will give you the nourishment needs to keep you healthier and more joyful. Here is a general rule for what you ought to endeavor to eat:

- 1 serving of organic product or veggies at each supper. Veggies and organic products also offer a touch of protein, starches, and plant-sourced fiber.

- 1 serving of lean protein at each feast. (vegetables, lean meats, low-fat dairy.) Vegetables and low-fat dairy offers a few sugars.

- 2 servings of starches for every day. (yams and entire oats are less handled and superior to entire wheat.)

- A touch of healthy fats like olive and canola oils, avocados, nuts. Nuts give a few starches just as healthy fats.

5. Consider your nourishment decisions.
At each supper, stop yourself, and inquire as to why you need to place unhealthy nourishments in your body.

A few purposes behind wandering from a healthy eating routine are:

- Healthy nourishment decisions are not accessible at gas stops.

- I'm eager now and I don't have the opportunity to run out/make a healthy supper.

A touch of arranging at the supermarket could help keep this from happening:

- Purchase hacked veggies like cleaved lettuce and infant carrots for a brisk serving of mixed greens.

- Purchase nuts or sunflower seeds for a fast fiber/protein/healthy fats help. You can add them to your plate of mixed greens for an additional crunch.

- Numerous natural products are versatile like bananas and apples.

6. Fight off sweet desires.

This can appear to be an unfavorable undertaking to certain individuals. In addition to the fact that we become connected to nourishments since it gives us comfort (like mother's chocolate chip treats), once your body is in an unhealthy cycle, handled nourishments like white sugar play hormonal ruin on your body and the wanting for desserts cycle becomes self-sustaining. When you're battling your body to end the sweet yearnings, this can cause us to feel like we're not in charge of what we eat, which can bring down self-esteem. If for some reason, you have desires for something sugar-loaded, here are a few hints to wean yourself off of that white sugar:

Need something sweet toward the beginning of the day? Supplant your cake, sugar-loaded grain, and espresso cake with oats beat with Stevia, cinnamon, natural product, and milk. If you don't care for oats (a few people don't care for the mush factor), attempt earthy colored rice.

Need an evening shot of sugar? Attempt a few dates and nuts.

Need an after-supper dessert? Attempt two or three squares of dull chocolate (pick the brand with minimal measure of sugar) and nutty spread. Need to include somewhat more pleasantness? Liquefy your chocolate, mix in the nutty spread, and include some agave nectar or Stevia. Not sweet enough? You can also blend in certain raisins to expand the yum factor even more, but when necessary.

7. Get your body going.
Setting aside some effort to go to the rec center may appear to be infeasible for caught up with working mothers and fathers. That is alright. You don't need to go to the exercise center to be fit as a fiddle. It's important to have more vitality, feel better, battle sickness, and

have the option to stay aware of the requests of your bustling life. There are even schedules accessible that are ten minutes or less. You can do these schedules each day since they won't exhaust the body. Here are a couple of instances of fast yet successful exercise programs:

Daily Workouts Fitness Trainer Free: This is a downloadable application accessible on apple store. https://apps.apple.com/us/app/daily-workouts-fitness-trainer/id469068059

Chatelaine Ten Minute Fitness: This downloadable application from iTunes is a global smash hit. https://itunes.apple.com/ca/app/chatelaine-10-minute-fitness/id643853756?mt=8

The 7 Min Workout: This site reveals to you which basic activities to do and times your whole seven-minute meeting for you. It's so quick, you don't have the opportunity to illuminate the word minute. Also, it offers the 7 Min diet if you offer your first name and email address. http://www.7-min.com/

Caution: These exercises are short, however, they can be thorough. Along these lines, it's ideal to check with your PCP if you have a condition you are being treated for, or whether you are over forty.

8. Remain well-prepped.
It may sound odd, however, brushing your teeth, washing up, styling your hair, wearing attire that is open to giving yourself a nail treatment, and dealing with your body all in all lifts your self-esteem.

If you truly feel better and put forth attempts to keep up your appearance, realizing you smell extraordinary in your preferred fragrance or cologne, or that your hair is delicate and touchable, or your eyes look more green since you're wearing your preferred green shirt can give you a lift for the afternoon.

Finding Appropriate Therapy

1. Go to treatment to support your self-esteem.
If you are experiencing difficulty with raising your self-esteem or want to see faster improvement, think about going to a proficient treatment. Successful treatment has appeared to have a huge impact on raising self-esteem.

You may also need to find support in keeping your journal, so you understand that there are subjects that you can't confront, or in the likelihood that you are attempting to confront them, they set you back enough to cause a disturbance in your life as you delve back on them.

Also, if you have a psychological issue like melancholy, anxiety, or different sorts of disarranges, this can affect your self-esteem. Getting treatment for a psychological issue can improve in an amazing nature.

2. Attempt Cognitive Behavioral Therapy.
Cognitive behavioral therapy (CBT) has been demonstrated to be powerful at developing self-esteem. CBT addresses programmed negative musings. These musings are the considerations that happen like a reflex when confronted with life circumstances.

For instance, if an individual with low self-esteem needs to prepare for a test in school, the individual may say, "I don't have a clue why I'm irritating. I'll get an F at any rate."

While experiencing CBT treatment, the therapist, who will be a guide or clinician, works in partnership with the customer to change those programmed beliefs. The advocate may propose testing the customer's theory—the customer will bomb regardless of how hard the customer examines. Help the customer with time management, stress abilities, and track progress until the understudy steps through the exam.

Different strategies utilized for CBT are unwinding methods (breathing activities), representation (mental practicing), and experiencing youth encounters to distinguish where the negative musings began. Recognizing the root of the negative contemplations forestalls self-esteem 'relapses'.

CBT is useful for people who don't have complex issues. Besides, CBT is useful for treating a few kinds of issues like discouragement and anxiety.

CBT may also be unreasonably organized for certain individuals.

3. Find psychodynamic treatment.
With psychodynamic therapy, treatment plans are custom-fitted to every individual and their individual needs. In a psychodynamic meeting, the customer is permitted to investigate all issues emerging for that day. The clinician enables the customer to search for conduct, thought, and emotional examples identified with that issue. Youth issues and occasions are frequently investigated to enable the customer to see how the past influences them and connects to their present.

For individuals who have complex issues or might want an individualized arrangement customized to their requirements, psychodynamic treatment may be better than CBT.

Psychodynamic treatment is a powerful method to use with an assortment of conditions and with patients with issues of changing unpredictability.

Distinguishing Low Self-Esteem

1. Know the potential impacts of low self-esteem.
Having low self-esteem doesn't simply impact your emotional state at some random second; it can have a long-running impact on your life. Understanding the potential impacts of low self-esteem may help inspire you to improve your viewpoint now. Low self-esteem may lead individuals to do any of the following:

- Endure injurious connections since they believe they are meriting the treatment or don't merit better treatment.

- Bully or misuse others.

- Being hesitant to take on objectives, destinations, or dreams since they don't think they can accomplish them.

- Become sticklers to compensate for their apparent blemishes.

- Continuously feel self-cognizant around others, be excessively distracted with their appearance, or imagine that others consider them.

- Continually search for markers that others don't care for them or ineffectively consider them.

- Think they are an act of futility.

- Have a low limit for stress.

Disregard their cleanliness or take part in activities that hurt their body, for example, drinking unnecessary liquor, smoking tobacco, or endeavoring self-destruction.

2. Pinpoint the base of your self-esteem issue.
Usually, low self-esteem begins with outer occasions. Individuals are not brought into the world with low self-esteem. It starts with our necessities not being met, negative feedback from others, or believing that a negative life occasion is our flaw.

For instance, children may reprimand themselves for their parent's separation or guardians feel powerless to enable their children to process their emotions.

Children who experience childhood in destitution and offspring of minorities are frequently at higher risk for growing low self-esteem.

3. Comprehend the low self-esteem cycle.
At the point when children (or adults) initially start to scrutinize their value, it is feasible for others or life occasions to fortify the negative sentiments, which can harden self-convictions that lead to low self-esteem.

4. Recollect how your parents treated you.
Guardians have been found to have the most grounded effect on people's self-esteem. Children's impressions of themselves are shaped with the assistance of their folks. There are a few unique sorts of parental practices that add to low self-esteem.

Frequently, when children are brought up in a severe home that doesn't give them emotional help, their self-esteem suffers. At the point when children and adults have emotional help, their emotional needs are met. Emotional help can be appeared from various per-spectives, for example, saying, "I love you", or "I'm glad for you"; helping kids with their sentiments and emotions, and how to adapt, and simply being there for them.

Emotional requirements are genuine necessities individuals have as they develop, along with physical (nourishment and drink) and men-tal (learning, critical thinking, and training) needs. Focusing on emo-tional necessities, just as physical and mental needs, assists children with feeling acknowledged and regarded.

5. Perceive cases of disgrace in your life.
Shaming is a typical child-bearing apparatus to help control the con-duct of children. For example, open disgracing of children via web-based networking media has become normal. Disgracing happens when somebody, for example, a guardian, parent, instructor, or other powerful figures, or different friends, causes you to feel like you are a horrendous individual for carrying on in a specific way or commit-ting an error.

For instance, and if for some reason, you don't show up on time to your work, your manager may cause you to feel embarrassed if he says, "You are not a dependable individual", as opposed to, "You have to come into work before. Take a stab at showing up to work thirty minutes sooner. If anything turns out badly, you'll have that extra time."

While disgracing is socially acknowledged, it is an injurious conduct, and frequently happens with other harsh practices that produce the sentiment of being disgraced. For instance, creator Beverly Engel re-views her mom hitting her before her neighbors, or rebuffing her with open presentations of shouting when she committed an error. These rates delivered sentiments of disgrace.

6. Distinguish maltreatment in past connections.
Harsh relationship designs are regularly the reason for low self-esteem. Patterns like scolding, deprecating, controlling, shouting, or reprimanding would all be able to add to people's contemplations of themselves. After some time, when these practices are rehashed again and again, the casualty may accept this negative information.

Harsh connections can also influence adults. The connections we have in adulthood frequently mirror our youthful connections. Relationship designs are shaped in youth, which influences our desires for our future connections.

7. Recognize occasions of horrible showing from before.
At the point when people reliably perform inadequately at an errand, at school, or an occupation, this can prompt lost self-esteem. It has been found over many years of research examinations that an industrious, however moderate, interface between poor scholarly execution and low self-esteem.

This isn't unexpected, considering the school is part of the greater part of our lives and for a larger part of our childhoods during our early stages in life.

8. Comprehend the impact of life occasions on your self-esteem.
Life occasions—even ones that are outside one's ability to control—frequently impact self-esteem. Job misfortune, monetary troubles, a separation, physical and psychological maladjustment, constant torment, and handicaps are kinds of circumstances that can be incessantly stressful and erode at a person's self-esteem.

Separation, occasions that produce injury like being in a vehicle or work mishap, being the survivor of an assault, or the demise of a relative or companion, can influence self-esteem too.

Money related stress and living in a financially discouraged zone can also influence self-esteem.

9. Survey your encounters of social acknowledgment.
Social acknowledgment, or the measure of dismissal encounters, has been found to have consequences for self-esteem. This has been found when contrasting the jobless with the utilized, yet different impacts like having a social disgrace (liquor abuse, psychological maladjustment), have been found to influence self-esteem.

10. Realize that your assessment of your physical appearance is associated with your self-esteem.
Physical appearance can influence one's self-esteem. It has been uncovered through research that there is an acknowledged definition for magnificence. While these standards are socially impacted, there is a socially acknowledged thought for excellence.

If an individual gets a great deal of dismissal or acknowledgment for their appearance, this could have an impact on a person's self-worth.

Research has discovered that when people assess their physical appearance, it is reliably slanted towards the negative and may not definitively reflect our true qualities. So it goes without saying, most people are too critical of their physical looks.

11. Note situations of bullying in your past.

Because of the persistent harassment, bullying adds to low self-esteem. There are repercussions to self-esteem for both the victim and the bully in this vicious cycle.

Recipients of bullying often have to live for years with the memories of them being bullied. They often feel humiliated about the abuse and assaults.

Most bullies also suffer from low self-esteem and feel more behind the wheel when they victimize others.

CHAPTER 18

HOW TO DEVELOP SELF-ESTEEM

Our self-esteem is imparted in us during our childhood. Being continually criticized by family, companions, and society will gradually strip us of our sentiments of self-worth. Our low self-esteem strips us of the self-confidence to settle on even the littlest of choices. These emotions don't need to be perpetual. Improving your self-esteem builds your confidence and is an initial move towards discovering satisfaction and a superior life.

Recognizing Your Self-Esteem

1. Self-esteem
Self-esteem, or how we feel about ourselves, is a significant part of our passionate prosperity. High self-esteem implies that we adore and acknowledge ourselves for just the way we are, and for the most part feel fulfilled more often than not. Low self-esteem implies that we are simply not content with the reflection we see in the mirror.

The Center for Clinical Interventions portrays people with low self-esteem as having profound situated, fundamental, negative convictions about themselves and the sort of individual they are. These convictions are frequently taken as realities or facts about their identity.

Untreated low-self-esteem can frequently prompt long-lasting issues like being the casualty of oppressive connections, feeling continually self-cognizant, and being so terrified of disappointment that you don't attempt to set objectives.

2. Access your self-esteem.
Realizing that you have low self-esteem is the initial step to improving and beating that psychological propensity. You may have low self-esteem if you have negative musings about yourself. These contemplations can rotate around one explicit attribute, for example, your weight or self-perception, or it can include numerous parts of your life, career, and connections.

In a situation, where your inward voice or contemplations about yourself are generally basic, you will likely have low self-esteem.

In the event, that your inward voice is positive and soothing, you will have higher self-esteem.

3. Tune in to your internal voice.
At the point when you have musings about yourself, decide if they are positive or negative. If you experience difficulty assessing this or seeing a theme, have a go at recording considerations you have about yourself consistently for a couple of days or even seven days. At that point look at the announcements for examples or inclinations.

The internal voice of somebody with low self-esteem frequently shows in one of the accompanying personas: a nagger, a generalist, a comparer, a catastrophizer, or a psyche reader. Every one of these special internal voices either affronts you or accepts the most noticeably awful image of you.

Hushing the negative internal voice is an initial phase in building your confidence. Supplanting it with positive musings will be the following objective.

For instance, your inward voice may say, "I didn't land the position I applied for, so I will never have an occupation again and I am futile." You need to change that to: "I am disillusioned about not landing this position, however, I have tried sincerely and the correct activity is out there hanging tight for me; I simply need to discover it."

4. Explore the wellspring of your brought down self-esteem.
No one has intrinsically low self-esteem from birth; it works from youth because of requirements not being met, negative input from others, or because of a significant negative life occasion. Knowing the wellspring of your self-esteem issues can assist you in defeating them.

In the event, that you saw a specific theme while assessing your internal voice, attempt to follow those sentiments back to your first memory about them.

For instance, if your pessimism is about your weight or appearance, attempt to recollect when you originally began feeling awkward with your weight; was it because of a specific remark or gathering of remarks?

5. Set an objective to improve your self-esteem.
The way to creating self-esteem is to divert your internal voice from a negative, basic voice to a positive, empowering voice. At last, you should choose to place in crafted by re-confining the manner, in which you consider yourself. Defining an underlying objective to be positive about yourself will put you on the way to more noteworthy self-confidence and self-adequacy.

For instance, your objective might be, "I will be more positive about myself and converse with myself like a companion as opposed to an adversary."

Improving Your Self-Care

1. Your positive qualities.
Concentrate on the things that you like about yourself to advise yourself that there is a whole other world to you than the negative musings your inward voice centers around. Salute yourself for your achievements without qualifying them.

Individuals with higher self-esteem can acknowledge that they have positive qualities, regardless of whether they are not perfect.

Post your rundown someplace obvious, similar to your washroom mirror, and look at it day by day. You can add to it as your inward voice turns out to be more positive.

2. Keep an energy journal.
Record your achievements, praises people give you, and great considerations you have about yourself. While the negative contemplations may not leave, investing more energy concentrating on the positive will improve your general sentiments of self-worth.

Journaling can be a useful asset to screen your internal discourse and improve your self-esteem.

Attempt to concentrate your energy journal on contradicting your ordinary negative inward musings. For instance, if you would affront yourself for not expressing your genuine thoughts about something, make sure to record times that you do express your real thoughts.

3. Utilize your journal for an objective setting.

You can set objectives for developing yourself without anticipating flawlessness in each part of your life. Your objectives ought to be clear and explicit, yet permit some 'squirm room' for blemish.

For instance, rather than, "I will consistently denounce people who are spreading separation," you may make your objective, "I will put forth a valiant effort to smoothly contradict the thoughts of other people who spread segregation and despise."

Rather than, "I will never eat sugar again and will shed thirty pounds," your objective could be, "I will endeavor to carry on with a more beneficial lifestyle with better nourishment decisions and more exercise."

4. Pardon yourself for being blemished.
Recollect that you—which is similar to everybody—are human. You don't need to be immaculate to have high self-esteem. If you can acknowledge yourself as you seem to be, regardless of whether you are attempting to improve in certain zones. You will have a higher self-esteem.

Make a mantra for yourself, similar to 'that is alright, I'm marvelous in any case'.

For instance, if you lost your temper and hollered at your child at the recreation center, you can say to yourself, "I am not great, and I will take a shot at keeping my feelings in charge. I will apologize to my child for shouting and disclose to him about why I got furious. It's alright, I'm a magnificent mother in any case."

5. Look for counseling.

If you feel that you can't improve your self-esteem all alone, or if you become vexed while investigating the underlying foundations of your low self-esteem, you might need to see a specialist who can assist you with distinguishing and manage the underlying foundations of your self-esteem problems.

Cognitive Behavioral Treatment (CBT) is a methodology that will address your programmed negative contemplations about yourself and show you how to manage your feelings better.

For increasingly complex self-esteem issues, more inside and outside psychodynamic treatment might be a superior choice for managing the underlying foundations of your issues.

6. Take an interest in beneficent work.
Numerous individuals start to rest and have easy thoughts about themselves when they are adding to their very own reason outside necessities. Chipping in for a magnanimous association helps both the volunteer and the beneficiaries of the foundation: a genuine success win!

Discover an association that tends to a reason that you feel energetic about. Volunteer someplace with a companion or a gathering of companions; this will support the association (numerous hands make light work) and the experience might be agreeable.

Receiving a More Positive Lifestyle

1. Setting time aside for self-care.
It very well may be hard to set aside a few minutes for yourself, yet causing time to do things that cause you to feel loose and cheerful

can improve your self-esteem just as your efficiency at work and home.

Discover a side interest that causes you to feel better genuinely and intellectually. A few people find that yoga, bicycling, or running assists them with finding a quiet, focused inspiration.

2. Surround yourself with positive people.
In the event, that there are negative impacts throughout your life that cause you to feel serious about yourself, attempt to limit or dispense with the time you go through with them. Remember for your life, rather, people who are positive and bolster your positive self-contemplations.

Making your friends and family mindful of your self-esteem building excursion will urge them to go about as an emotionally supportive network for you.

You might need to tell dear companions or family something like, "I am chipping away at improving my self-esteem. You can help me by bringing up when I say something negative regarding myself with the goal that I am progressively mindful of my pessimism."

3. Having a healthy diet.
Picking nourishments that are nutritious and lower in sugar and fat can support your vitality, cut down on sugar crashes, and improve your general well-being.

Maintain a strategic distance from trend eating less carbs and settle on entire nourishments that are negligibly handled.

Keep away from nourishments like sweet treats, pop, cake, doughnuts, and baked goods, which lead to gigantic vitality crashes, potential cerebral pains, and offer no sustenance, conceivable sickness, and included calories.

4. Exercise more.
In any event, when setting off to the exercise center isn't a choice, an energetic walk is frequently all you need to move more and improve your well-being. A little exercise can give you more vitality, cause you to feel better, and help support your resistant framework.

Numerous people find that strolling outside is reviving and therapeutic, especially in the event that they invest the vast majority of their energy working inside.

Indeed, even a ten-minute exercise on more than one occasion each day offers advantages to your well-being.

5. Spend time on home cleanliness.
In the event that you put thought and energy into your appearance by choosing apparel that causes you to feel sure and set up while rehearsing everyday cleanliness propensities, you will feel progressively good and sure.

Relinquishing Perfection

1. Perceive inaccessible measures.
Like Picasso's artistic creations, flawlessness changes are subjective depending on each person's preferences. Flawlessness is an expression that is emotional and regularly self-forced. It's alright to hold yourself to better expectations, yet regularly, those measures are hopeful since life doesn't go as arranged. It is anything but difficult to get baffled when you can't coordinate our optimal picture of yourself.

This isn't an awful thing since this rouses people to improve, discover better and effective methods for getting things done, and be the most magnificent they can be.

2. Excuse yourself.
You can figure out how to keep this human inclination from getting useless by getting more sympathetic of yourself when things don't go the way you want or expect them, and to think strongly of ourselves by feeling great in our achievements and qualities so we can appreciate being what our identity is correct now in the present moment.

CONCLUSION

So we've finally come to the end of our voyage. Though it's been a considerably long one, I hope it's been worthwhile. Over the first section of this book, we've been able to get a grasp on understanding the idea of SELF-CONFIDENCE, how it affects us and we also considered in detail some techniques to help deal with it, such as ASSERTIVENESS, MEDITATION, POSITIVE THINKING, POSITIVE SELF IMAGE, and RESILIENCE. Then we also looked at how to handle a real-life cause of low self-confidence i.e. BULLYING.

And in Section 2, we proceeded to divert our attention to SELF-ESTEEM, what it's all about, managing CRITICISM, STRESS, and then an in-depth look into helpful techniques to beat low self-esteem such as RECOGNIZING AND MANAGING EMOTIONS, REFLECTIVE PRACTICES, and MINDFULNESS.

And last but not least, in Section 3 we looked at a hands-on step by step practical guide on dealing with some of the most reoccurring questions affiliated with our topic on how to; DEAL WITH CRITICISM, DEVELOPE SELF-ESTEEM, OVERCOME LOW SELF-ESTEEM, ACCEPT AND HANDLE MISTAKES, in no particular order.

The concept of self-confidence and self-esteem is so broad that for brevities sake, we could only cover so much in the scope of this book, but we hope to have laid the foundation to guide you on your journey. Here are a few pointers from the author that you should always remember;

- Always remind yourself that you are 'Good Enough' regardless of the circumstance.

- No one deserves to be bullied, speak out.

- Quit comparing yourself with others.

- You can achieve anything you set your mind to.

- Perspective matters e.g.: I'm not too short, he's just too tall.

- A smile is the best accessory you could have on, so don't lose it.

- Everyone doesn't have to like you, but you have to like you.

- Practice makes perfect.

And on this note, I'll bid you farewell.

Emma

REFERENCES

Bandura, A. (1997). Self-efficacy: The exercise of control. New York: Freeman. Google Scholar.

Cramer, R. J., Neal, T. M. S., & Brodsky, S. L. (2009). Self-efficacy and confidence: Theoretical distinctions and implications for trial consultation. Consulting Psychology Journal: Practice and Research, 61, 319–334. Google Scholar.

Dixon, T. (2007). Evolving self-confidence: How to become free from anxiety disorders and depression. Newton Aycliffe Co, Durham: Help-For.

Egan, G. (2007). The skilled helper: A problem-management and opportunity-development approach to helping, Eighth edition. Belmont, CA: Thompson Brooks/Cole.

Erev, I., Wallsten, T. S., & Budescu, D. V. (1994). Simultaneous over- and under-confidence: The role of error in the judgment process. Psychological Review, 101, 519–527. Google Scholar.

Gerber, S.K. (2003). Responsive therapy: A systematic approach to counseling skills. Boston: Houghton Mifflin Company/Lahaska Press.

Gigerenzer, G., Hoffrage, U., & Kleinbölting, H. (1991). Probabilistic mental models: A Brunswikian theory of confidence. Psychological Review, 98, 506–528. Google Scholar.

Glazer, M., & Weber, M. (2007). Overconfidence and trading volume. Geneva Risk and Insurance Review, 32, 1–36. Google Scholar.

Judge, T. A., & Bono, J. E. (2001). Relationship of core self-evaluations traits—self-esteem, generalized self-efficacy, locus of control, and emotional stability—with job satisfaction and job performance: A meta-analysis. Journal of Applied Psychology, 86, 80–92. Google Scholar.

Koellinger, P., Minniti, M., & Schade, C. (2007). I think I can, I think I can—Overconfidence and entrepreneurial behavior. Journal of Economic Psychology, 28(4), 502–527. Google Scholar.

Lerner, J. S., Gonzalez, R. M., Small, D. A., & Fischhoff, B. (2003). Effects of fear and anger o perceived risks of terrorism: A national field experiment. Psychological Science, 14, 144–150. Google Scholar.

Malmendier, U., & Tate, G. (2005). CEO overconfidence and corporate investment. Journal of Finance, 60(6), 2661–2700. Google Scholar.

McLeod, S. (2007). Maslow's hierarchy of needs. Retrieved May 06, 2016, from http://www.simplypsychology.org/maslow.html

McMahon, S. (1992). The portable therapist: Wise and inspiring answers to the questions people in therapy ask most. NY: Dell Publishing.

Moore, D. A., & Healy, P. J. (2008). The trouble with overconfidence. Psychological Review, 115, 502–517. Google Scholar.

Peterson, C. (2006). A primer in positive psychology. NY: Oxford University Press.

Rigal, E.A. (2015). Flawed: How to stop hating on yourself, others, and the things that make you who you are. NY: Perigee/Penguin Random house.

Roberts Jr., W.B. (2006). Bullying from both sides: Strategic interventions for working with bullies and victims. Thousand Oaks, CA: Corwin Press.

Rosengren, D.B. (2009). Building motivational interviewing skills: A practitioner workbook. NY: The Guilford Press.

Rufus, A. (2014). Unworthy: How to stop hating yourself. NY: Jeremy P. Tarcher/Penguin.

Seligman, L. (2006). Theories of counseling and psychotherapy: systems, strategies, and skills, Second edition. Upper Saddle River, NJ: Pearson/Merrill Prentice Hall.

Sheier, M. F., & Carver, C. S. (1992). Effect of optimism on psychological and physical well-being: Theoretical overview and empirical update. Cognitive Therapy and Research, 16, 201–228. Google Scholar.

Shrauger, J. S. (1972). Self-esteem and reactions to being observed by others. Journal of Personality and Social Psychology, 23, 192–200. Google Scholar.

Shrauger, J. S., & Schohn, M. (1995). Self-confidence in college students: Conceptualization measurement, and behavioral implications. Assessment, 2, 255–278. Google Scholar.

Slovic, P. (Ed.) (2001). Smoking: Risk, perception, and policy. Thousand Oaks, CA: Sage. Google Scholar.

Sporer, S. L., Pnrod, S., Reed, D., & Cutler, B. (1995). Choosing, confidence, and accuracy: A meta-analysis of the confidence-accuracy relation in eyewitness identification studies. Psychological Bulletin, 118(3), 315–327. Google Scholar.

Stone, H. & Stone, S. (1993). Embracing your inner critic. NY: Harper One/Harper Collins.

Welford, M. (2013). The power of self-compassion: Using compassion-focused therapy to end self-criticism and build self-confidence. Oakland: New Harbinger Publications, Inc.

Do not go yet; One Last Thing to Do

if you enjoyed this book or found it useful, I'd be very grateful if you'd post a short review on Amazon. Your support does make a difference, and I read all the reviews personally so I can get your feedback and make this book even better.

Thanks again for your support!

Remember to click here to access your free gift or scan the QR code below.

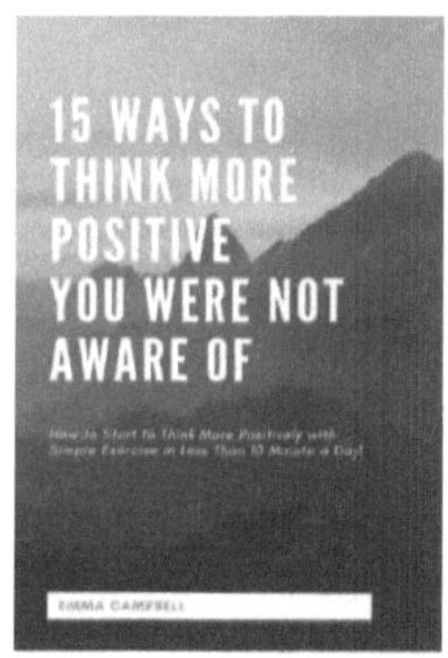

And if you want a better experience you can enjoy the audiobook for free here or you can scan the QR code below

www.ingramcontent.com/pod-product-compliance
Lightning Source LLC
Chambersburg PA
CBHW031055250726

48655CB00004B/1452